I0779200

The Itching Palm

A STUDY OF THE HABIT
OF TIPPING IN AMERICA

By

William R. Scott

AUTHOR OF
The Americans in Panama,
Scientific Circulation Management, Etc.

London
Spradabach Publishing
2023

Spradabach Publishing
BM Box Spradabach
London WC1N 3XX

The Itching Palm: A Study of the Habit of Tipping in America

First published in 1916
First Spradabach edition published 2023
© Spradabach Publishing 2023

Interior design by Alex Kurtagic

ISBN 978-1-909606-45-6

British Library Cataloguing-in-Publication Data:
A catalogue record for this book is available from the British Library.

HE AUTHOR WILL BE PLEASED TO CORRESPOND WITH ANY READER WHO APPROVES OF, OR HAS COMMENTS TO MAKE UPON, THE ATTITUDE TAKEN IN THE BOOK TOWARDS THE TIPPING CUSTOM.

WILLIAM R. SCOTT.
PADUCAH, KENTUCKY.

Table of Contents

Note on This Edition

The text in this volume is based on the Penn Publishing Company's edition of *The Itching Palm* by William R. Scott, published in Philadelphia in 1916. It is herein reproduced in its entirety.

The spelling, punctuation, and capitalisation appear as in the original. The titles of books referred to in the text, however, have been set in italics. Extensive quotes have been set as block quotes.

A small number of editorial footnotes have been added and a new index has been generated.

I

Flunkyism in America

"Oliver Cromwell struck a mortal blow at the universal heart of Flunkyism," wrote Carlyle of the execution of Charles I.

Yet, Flunkyism is not dead!

In the United States alone more than 5,000,000 persons derive their incomes, in whole or in part, from "tips," or gratuities. They have the moral malady denominated The Itching Palm.

Tipping is the modern form of Flunkyism. Flunkyism may be defined as a willingness to be servile for a consideration. It is democracy's deadly foe. The two ideas cannot live together except in a false peace. The tendency always is for one to sap the vitality of the other.

1

The full significance of the foregoing figures is realized in the further knowledge that these 5,000,000 persons with itching palms are fully 10 per cent. of our entire industrial population; for the number of persons engaged in gainful occupations in this country is less than 50,000,000.

Whether this constitutes a problem for moralists, economists and statesmen depends upon the ethical appraisement of tipping. If tipping is moral, the interest is reduced to the economic phase—whether the remuneration thus given is normal or abnormal. If tipping is immoral, the fact that 5,000,000 Americans practice it constitutes a problem of first rate importance.

Accurate statistics are not obtainable, but conservative estimates place the amount of money given in one year by the American people in tips, or gratuities, at a figure somewhere between $200,000,000 and $500,000,000![1]

Now we have the full statement of the case against tipping—five million persons receiving in excess of two hundred millions of dollars for—what?

It will be interesting to examine the ethics, economics and psychology of tipping to determine whether the American people receive a value for this expenditure.

---

1   In 2011, Ofer H. Azar estimated that Americans were by then tipping $47,000,000,000 per year. 'Business strategy and the social norm of tipping', *Journal of Economic Psychology*, Volume 32, Issue 3, June 2011, Pages 515-525.

II

On Personal Liberty

he Itching Palm is a moral disease. It is as old as the passion of greed in the human mind. Milton was thinking of it when he exclaimed:

Help us to save free conscience from the paw,
Of hireling wolves whose gospel is their maw.

Although it had only a feeble lodgment in the minds of the Puritans, because their minds were in the travail that gave birth to democracy, enough remained to perpetuate the disease. In Europe, under monarchical ideals, a person could accept a tip without feeling the acute loss of self-respect that attends the practice in America, under democratic ideals. For tipping is essentially an aristocratic custom.

Tipping Un-American

If it seems astounding that this aristocratic practice should reach such stupendous proportions in a republic, we must remember that the same republic allowed slavery to reach stupendous proportions.

If Tipping is Un-American, Some Day, Somehow, It Will Be Uprooted Like African Slavery

Apparently the American conscience is dormant upon this issue. But this is more apparent than real. The people are stirring vaguely and uneasily over the ethics of the custom. Six State Legislatures reflected the dawning of a new conscience by considering in their 1915 sessions bills relating to tipping. They were Wisconsin, Illinois, Iowa, Nebraska, Tennessee and South Carolina.

The geographical distribution of these States is significant. It is proof that the opposition to the practice is not isolated, not sectional, but national. North, Central, South, the verdict was registered that tipping is wrong. The South, former home of slavery, might be supposed to be favorable to this aristocratic custom. On the contrary the most vigorous opposition to it is found there. Mississippi, Arkansas, Tennessee, and South Carolina simultaneously had laws against tipping—with the usual contests in the courts on their constitutionality.

The Negro was servile by law and inheritance. The modern tip-taker voluntarily assumes, in a republic where he is actually and theoretically equal to all other citizens, a servile attitude for a fee. While the form of servitude is different, the slavery is none the less real in the case of the tip-taker.

Strangely enough, bills to prohibit tipping often have been vetoed by Governors—notably in Wisconsin—on the ground that they curtailed personal liberty. That is to say, a bill which removed the chains of social slavery from the serving classes was declared to be an abridgment of liberty! "Oh, Liberty, how many crimes are committed in thy name!"

The Legislature in Wisconsin almost re-passed the bill over the Governor's veto. In Tennessee and Kentucky bills have been vetoed for the same given reason, though Tennessee in 1916 finally had such a law in force. In Illinois, the law was framed primarily with the object of preventing the leasing of privileges to collect tips in hotels and other public places, and not against the individual giver or taker of tips.

Short-Lived Laws

The courts have negatived such laws on much the same grounds, so that anti-tipping laws thus far have been, generally, short-lived. The reason is, of course, that popular sentiment has not been behind the laws in an extent sufficient to give them power. Judges and executives simply have yielded to their own class impulses, and the pressure from organized interests, to suppress the legislation. When the public conscience finds itself and becomes organized and articulate, they will have no difficulty in finding grounds for declaring regulatory laws constitutional. The history of the prohibition of the liquor business is a parallel.

PERSONAL LIBERTY

Personal liberty is a phrase that is being redefined in America in every decade. In its broadest sense it is interpreted to mean that a man has the right to go to perdition if he so elects without neighbors or the government taking note or interfering.

Anti-liquor laws in the early days of the temperance movement fared badly from this interpretation, just as anti-tipping laws fare to-day. But as public sentiment crystallized, and judges and executives began to feel the pressure at the polls, a new conception of personal liberty developed. In its present accepted sense, as regards liquor, it is interpreted to mean that no citizen may act or live in a way that is detrimental to himself, his neighbor or his government, and his privilege to drink liquor is abridged or abolished at will.

The right to give tips is not inalienable. It is not grounded on personal liberty. If the public conscience reaches the conviction that tipping is detrimental to democracy, that it destroys that fineness of self-respect requisite in a republic, the right will be abridged or withdrawn.

III

Barbary Pirates

he American people became fully aroused on one occasion to the iniquity of tipping—on an international scale.

In 1801 President Jefferson decided that the United States could tolerate no longer the system of tribute enforced by the Barbary States along the shores of the Mediterranean.

Before our action, no European government had made more than fitful, ineffectual attempts to break up a practice at once humiliating to national honor and disastrous to national commerce. Candor requires the admission that we, too, submitted for years to this system of paying tribute to Barbary pirates for an unmolested passage of our ships, but the significant fact is that American manhood did finally and successfully revolt against the practice.

By 1805 our naval forces had brought the pirates to their knees and all Europe breathed grateful sighs of relief. Even the Pope commended the American achievement. The practice was contrary to every dictate of self-respect.

TRIBUTE

These pirates of Algiers, Tunis, Morocco and Tripoli did not pretend to have any other right behind their demands for tribute than the right they could enforce with cutlass and cannon—a right ferociously employed. It was not robbery in the ordinary sense of the word. They demanded a fee based on the value of the cargo for the privilege of sailing in the Mediterranean, and this being paid, the ship could proceed to its destination. Ship-owners soon began to figure tribute as a fixed expense of navigation, like insurance, and passed the added cost along to the ultimate consumer.

This practice of paying tribute was a system of international tipping. The Barbary pirates granted immunity to those who obeyed the custom, but made it decidedly warm and expensive for those who dared to protest against it—just as do our modern pirates in hotels, sleeping cars, restaurants, barber shops and elsewhere.

If a ship refused to pay tribute it was sunk, and the sailors went to slavery in the desert, or to death by fearful torture. President Jefferson could not see any basis of right in the position of the Barbary States that the Mediterranean was their private lake through which ships could not pass without paying toll. He sent Decatur to register our protest.

With the Pinckney slogan: "MILLIONS FOR DEFENSE—NOT ONE CENT FOR TRIBUTE!" the American naval forces made good our position. The tips that skippers of our nation had been paying to the pirates were saved and the custom soon was abandoned by other nations.

* * *

To-day, the old battle cry is reversed to read: "Millions for tribute—not one cent for defense!"

It is certain that a greater tribute is paid in one week in the United States in the form of tips, than our merchantmen paid during the whole period that they knuckled to the Barbary pirates.

In New York City alone more than $100,000 a day is paid in gratuities to waiters, hotel employes, chauffeurs, barbers and allied classes. But New York has reached a subserviency to the tipping custom that is amazing in a democratic country.

This vast tribute is paid for not more real service than the Barbary pirates rendered to those from whom they exacted tribute. It is given to workers who are paid by their employers to perform the services enjoyed by the public. If the Barbary pirates could see the ease with which a princely tribute is exacted from a docile public by the tip-takers, they would yearn to be reincarnated as waiters in America—the Land of the Fee!

IV

Personnel and Distribution

he Itching Palm is not limited to the serving classes. It is found among public officials, where it is particularized as grafting, and it is found among store buyers, purchasing agents, traveling salesmen and the like, and takes the form of splitting commissions. There are varied manifestations of the disease, but whether the amount of the gratuity is ten cents to a waiter or $10,000 to a captain of police, the practice is the same.

This is a partial list of those affected:

Baggagemen
Barbers

13

Bartenders
Bath attendants
Bell-boys
Bootblacks
Butlers
Cab drivers
Chauffeurs
Charwomen
Coachmen
Cooks
Door men
Elevator men
Garbage men
Guides
Hat-boys
Housekeepers
Janitors
Maids
Manicurists
Messengers
Mail carriers
Pullman porters
Rubbish collectors
Steamship stewards
Theater attendants
Waiters

The foregoing list is not offered as a complete roster of those who regularly or occasionally receive tips. Nearly every one can think of additions, and at Christmas the list is extended to include money gifts to policemen, delivery men and numerous others.

THE TIP-TAKING CLASSES

At the last Census, in 1910, there were 38,167,336 persons in the United States, out of a total population of ninety-odd millions, who were engaged in gainful occupations, that is, who worked for specified wages or salaries. Of this number, 3,772,174 persons were engaged in domestic or personal service, or practically ten per cent. of the industrial population.

This means that in round numbers 4,000,000 Americans of both sexes and all ages were engaged in the lines of work specified in the foregoing list, with certain additions as mentioned. These are the citizens who profit by the tipping practice.

Since 1910 the growth in population to one hundred millions, and the steadily widening spread of the tipping practice will increase the beneficiaries of tipping to 5,000,000. An idea of the relative distribution of the total may be obtained from the statistics of fifty leading cities. The numbers represent the tip-taking classes in each city.

City	Number	City	Number
Albany	8,000	Minneapolis	19,000
Atlanta	23,000	Nashville	15,000
Baltimore	48,000	New Haven	9,000

City	Number	City	Number
Birmingham	16,000	New Orleans	37,000
Boston	61,000	New York	400,000
Bridgeport	5,200	Newark	17,000
Buffalo	25,000	Oakland	11,000
Cambridge	7,500	Omaha	10,000
Chicago	135,000	Paterson	5,000
Cincinnati	30,000	Philadelphia	105,000
Cleveland	31,000	Pittsburgh	41,000
Columbus	14,000	Portland	17,000
Dayton	6,500	Providence	14,000
Denver	17,000	Richmond	15,000
Detroit	26,000	Rochester	13,000
Fall River	4,000	St. Louis	56,000
Grand Rapids	5,500	St. Paul	16,000
Indianapolis	19,000	San Francisco	44,000
Jersey City	14,000	Scranton	6,000
Kansas City	24,000	Seattle	19,000
Los Angeles	26,000	Spokane	7,000
Lowell	5,500	Syracuse	9,000
Louisville	23,000	Toledo	9,500
Memphis	19,000	Washington	43,000
Milwaukee	22,000	Worcester	9,000

In all other cities, towns and hamlets there are proportionate quotas to bring the grand total to 5,000,000. Any estimate of the daily tipping tribute for the whole country necessarily is only an approximation, but $600,000 is a conservative figure. At this rate the annual tribute is around $220,000,000.

IN NEW YORK ALONE

Taking New York with its 400,000 persons who profit from tipping, the leading classes of beneficiaries are as follows:

Barbers	20,000
Bartenders	12,000
Bell-boys	2,500
Bootblacks	3,500
Chauffeurs	12,000
Janitors	25,000
Manicurists	4,500
Messengers	1,500
Porters	15,000
Waiters	35,000

The tipping to these and other classes varies both in amount and regularity. Waiters and manicurists in the better-class places receive no pay from their employers and depend entirely upon tips for their compensation. Barbers and chauffeurs are classes which receive wages and supplement them with tips. Sometimes the employer will pay wages and require that all tips be turned in to the house.

It is a common feature of the "Help Wanted" columns to state that the job is desirable to the workers because of "good tips." Thus the employers are fully alert to the economic advantage of tipping, and wherever it is practicable they throw upon their patrons the entire cost of servant hire.

The extent to which employers are exploiting the public is realized vaguely, if at all. The vein of generosity and the fear of violating a social convention can be worked profitably, and they are in league with their employees to make it assay the maximum amount to the patron.

In a restaurant where the employer has thus shifted the cost of waiter hire to the shoulders of the public, the patron who conscientiously objects to tipping has not the slightest chance in the world of a square deal in competition with the patron who pays tribute, although he pays as much for the food.

A waiter, knowing that his compensation depends upon what he can work out of his patron, employs every art to stimulate the tipping propensity, from subtle flattery to out-right bull-dozing. He weaves a spell of obligation around a patron as tangible, if invisible, as the web a spider weaves around a fly. He plays as consciously upon the patron's fear of social usage as the musician in the alcove plays upon his violin.

This is a particularly bad ethical and economic situation from any viewpoint. The patron, getting only one service, pays two persons for it—the employer and the employee. The payment to the employer is fixed, but to the employee it is dependent upon the whim of the patron. To make this situation normal, the patron should pay only once, and this should cover both the cost of the food and the services of the waiter. Theoretically this is the present idea under the common law, but actually the patron is required, through fear of well-defined penalties, to pay twice.

Naturally, if the $200,000,000 or more annually given to those serving the public should be withdrawn suddenly, employers would face the necessity of a radical readjustment of wage systems. In many lines wages would be increased to a normal basis, either at the expense of the employer's profits, or through additional charges to patrons. Before going further into the employer phase of the practice, the economics of tipping in individual instances will be an interesting study.

The Economics of Tipping

he basic question is, does tipping represent a sound exchange of wealth? Do the American people receive full value, or any value, for the $200,000,000 or more given in tips?

Values, of course, may be sentimental as well as substantial and, so far as tipping is concerned, it can be demonstrated that if any values are received they are sentimental. The satisfaction of giving, the balm to vanity, the indulgence of pride, are the values obtained by the giver of a tip in exchange for his money.

It is a stock argument for tipping that the person serving frequently performs extra services, or displays special painstaking, which deserve extra compensation. Only an examination of individual instances can determine whether this is true. The proportion of the tipping tribute which really pays for extraordinary service is negligible. A brief inquiry into a few of the more prominent instances of tipping follows.

THE WAITER

If food is sold undelivered, then the waiter in bringing it to the patron and assisting him in its consumption does perform an extra service for which payment is due.

But this is not the fact, any more than that a shoe clerk should be tipped for assisting a customer in the selection of his employer's footwear. In both instances, the cost of the service is included in the price of the article—food or shoes.

The prices on the bill of fare have been figured to include all costs of serving it, such as cook-hire, waiter-hire, rent, music, table ware, raw materials and overhead charges. If a sirloin steak costs seventy-five cents a definite part of that amount represents the wages of the waiter serving it.

Thus the waiter has no claim upon the patron for compensation, because the patron, in paying for the food, provides the proprietor with funds from which the waiter's wages will be paid. If the patron, in addition, gives the waiter a tip it is clearly a gift for which no value has been returned. The waiter is paid twice for one service.

ECONOMIC WASTE

The question then recurs, is this gift to the waiter a sound economic transaction? Economists teach that no transaction is industrially sound which does not involve an equal exchange of values. The exchange of five dollars for a pair of shoes is a sound transaction because the dealer and the customer each receive a value. But the gift of a quarter to a waiter as a tip is an unsound transaction because the patron receives nothing in return—nothing of like substantiality.

The patron may justify the gift from sentimental considerations, of pride, generosity or fear of violating a social convention, but no sophistry of reasoning can prove that a substantial value has been received.

Of course, a waiter may give a patron more than the proprietor agrees to give in the bill of fare, and this undoubtedly is an extra service—but it is also a dishonest service. Every extra service to one patron means a deficiency of service to other patrons. It is a common experience that liberal tipping obtains special attentions which non-tipping patrons miss, but, being dishonest, such a condition is outside the scope of this inquiry. When a patron pays for food he is entitled to adequate and equal service, and no largess by other patrons should interfere with this basic right.

On its economic side, then, tipping is wrong. Wealth is exchanged without both parties to the transaction receiving fair values. The psychology and ethics of the transaction will be considered in other chapters.

THE BARBER

No tipping is so inexcusable as that which is done to a barber. The trade is highly organized and the workers are well paid under good working conditions. There is not the slightest chance for the barber to serve a patron in a way for which the patron does not pay in the shop tariffs.

If a haircut costs thirty-five cents, the patron is entitled to just as good a hair-cut as the barber can give. The patron enters the shop upon the assumption that he is entitled to a satisfactory service. Hence, in tipping a barber a patron is yielding in a peculiarly timid way to the mesmeric influence which the tipping custom exerts over its devotees.

It is a wanton waste of wealth, an unsound business transaction, because money is given where charity is unnecessary and where absolutely nothing is given in return. "But my barber takes lots of pains with my hair," the patron exclaims in justification of the tip. As in the instance of the waiter, if he takes more than a normal amount of pains with your hair he is dishonest to his employer and to other patrons whom he must neglect to pay you special attention. Your right is to a satisfactory service, and this you pay for in the regular charge.

Any extra compensation is unearned increment to the barber.

The unctuous manner he employs to arouse a sense of obligation in a patron, when stripped of disguises, is a plain hold-up game. This will be shown in the consideration of the psychology and ethics of tipping.

THE HOTEL

The attitude that hotel employees have been allowed to develop toward the public is a blot upon professional hospitality.

Every one of them takes the hotel patron for fair game. And the hotel proprietor, with a few notable exceptions, encourages this despicable attitude. The assumption is that the patron pays at the desk only for the privilege of being in the building.

Hence, they will not cheerfully move his baggage to his room unless he pays to get it there. He cannot have a pitcher of ice water without being made to feel that he owes for the service. The maid who cares for his room exacts her toll. The head waiter demands payment for showing him to a seat. The individual waiters at each meal (and they are changed each meal by the head-waiter so that the patron has a new tip to give each time he dines) require fees. If he rings a bell, asks any assistance, goes out the door to a cab, in short, whichever way he turns, an itching palm is outstretched!

Just think for a moment of the real significance of this state of affairs. Hotel hospitality? Why, the Barbary pirates would have been ashamed to go it that strong!

To ignore this grafting spirit means insulting annoyance. The suave hotel manager listens to your complaint and smiles assurance that his guests shall have proper service, but underneath the smile he has a contempt for the "tight-wad," and instructs the cashier always to give the waiters small change so as to make tipping easy for the patrons.

In truth, what does a hotel guest pay for when he registers? Certainly for the service of the bell-boy who carries his suit-case to his room; for the keeping of the room in order; for water, clean towels and other necessities for his comfort; for the privilege of finding a seat in the dining room; for the right to use the doors—all without extra charge.

But the hotel manager admits this in theory and outrageously violates it in practice. All tipping done to bell-boys, porters, maids, waiters, door men, hat-boys and other servitors in a hotel is sheer economic waste. When the guest pays his bill at the desk he pays for all the service they perform.

The hotel manager protests that the money that passes between his guests and his employees is not his affair. But he proves his insincerity by adjusting his wage scale on the estimate that the guests will pass money to his employees!

Professional hospitality as "enjoyed" by Americans is a travesty on democracy. That Europe should have such a system and spirit is historically understandable. Tipping, and the aristocratic idea it exemplifies, is what we left Europe to escape. It is a cancer in the breast of democracy.

THE CHAUFFEUR

It would be possible to run through all the classes tipped and prove that the extra compensation is unearned. The chauffeur is a latter-day instance of the itching palm. Like the barber, the chauffeur is paid well for his work. He does nothing for which the patron should give him a tip. The taxi-meter charges the patron roundly for all the service given, yet tipping chauffeurs is as common in the larger cities as tipping barbers or waiters. It simply shows the spread of the practice to workers who have no other claim upon it than their own avaricious impulses—and the extreme docility of the public. Every tip given to a chauffeur is so clearly a bad economic transaction that further argument is unnecessary.

So widespread has the practice become that tipping is, individually, a problem, as well as collectively. The traveler has a formidable cost to face in the tipping required. When the total passes $200,000,000 a year, it becomes a problem which the American people will find more difficult of solution the longer it continues unchecked.

The whole argument is summed up in this. Tipping is an economic waste because it is double pay for one service—or pay for no service. It causes one person to give wealth to another without a fair return in values, or without any return. The pay that employers give to their employees should be the only compensation they receive. All the money given by the public on the side is unearned increment.

The best condition for a fair exchange of wealth is where standards are known and prices are definite. Self-respect and sound economics flourish in such an atmosphere, whereas, if values are hazy and compensation is indirect and irregular, as it is under the custom of tipping, the bickering that follows degrades manhood.

From an economic viewpoint, all businesses are on an abnormal basis which figure minimum wages, or no wages, to their employees on the assumption that the public will, through gratuities, pay for this item of service.

"One service—one compensation" is the only right relation of seller and buyer, of patron and proprietor.

VI

The Ethics of Tipping

The moral wrong of tipping is in the grafting spirit it engenders in those who profit by it; in the rigid class distinctions it creates in a republic; in the loss of that fineness of self-respect without which men and women are only so much clay—worthless dregs in the crucible of democracy.

In a monarchy it may be sufficient for self-respect to be limited to the governing classes; but the theory of Americanism requires that every citizen shall possess this quality. We grant the suffrage simply upon manhood—upon the assumption that all men are equal in that fundamental respect.

THE PRICE OF PRIDE

Hence, whatever undermines self-respect, manhood, undermines the republic. Whatever cultivates aristocratic ideals and conventions in a republic strikes at the heart of democracy. Where all men are equal, some cannot become superior unless the others grovel in the dust. Tipping comes into a democracy to produce that relation.

Tipping is the price of pride. It is what one American is willing to pay to induce another American to acknowledge inferiority. It represents the root of aristocracy budding anew in the hearts of those who publicly renounced the system and all its works.

The same Americans who profit by this undemocratic practice exert as much influence, proportionably, in the government of the republic, as those who give tips, or those whose sense of rectitude will not allow them to give or accept gratuities. Is a man who will take a tip as good a citizen, is his self-respect as fine, as the one who will not accept a tip, or who will not give a tip? Is the one as well qualified to vote as the other?

What is a gentleman? What is a lady?

Can a waiter be a gentleman? Can a maid be a lady?

Would a gentleman or a lady accept a gratuity?

What would happen if a tip should be offered to the average "gentleman" who patronizes restaurants, and taxicabs and barber shops? He would have a brainstorm of self-righteous wrath!

The Test of Democracy

And there is the test. If a "gentleman" would not accept a tip, is it gentlemanly to give a tip? If a "gentleman's" self-respect would rebel at the idea of accepting a gratuity, why should not a waiter's self-respect rebel at the idea?

"Oh, but there's a difference!"

The difference is there indeed. It is the difference between aristocracy and democracy. In an aristocracy a waiter may accept a tip and be servile without violating the ideals of the system. In the American democracy to be servile is incompatible with citizenship.

Every tip given in the United States is a blow at our experiment in democracy. The custom announces to the world that at heart we are aristocratic, that we do not believe practically that "all men are created equal"; that the class distinctions forbidden by our organic law are instituted through social conventions and flourish in spite of our lofty professions.

Unless a waiter can be a gentleman, democracy is a failure. If any form of service is menial, democracy is a failure. Those Americans who dislike self-respect in servants are undesirable citizens; they belong in an aristocracy.

Tips Disliked by Recipients

Fortunately, conditions are not as rotten as the extent of the tipping practice would indicate. The vast majority of Americans who give tips do so under duress. At heart they loathe the custom. They feel that it is tribute exacted as arbitrarily and unrighteously as the tribute paid to the Barbary pirates. Some day this majority will rise up and deal as summarily with the tipping practice as our forefathers dealt with the Mediterranean tribute custom!

A great number of servants and workers in such lines as barber shops, restaurants and other public service positions are equally opposed to the custom. They are caught up, however, in a system where they must conform to the custom or lose their employment. Many a barber or waiter or chauffeur whose self-respect rebels at taking a tip is forced to do so in order not to offend patrons. For nothing so stirs up a "gentleman" as for the person serving to decline a tip. The reason is that he feels the rebuke implied in the refusal and knows in his conscience that the practice is wrong. We always grow more indignant at a just accusation than at an unjust one!

CONSCIENCE IS STIRRING

The constant re-appearance of laws to regulate tipping, in every section of the country, proves that the conscience of the people is stirring. The daily and periodical press now and then condemn the practice editorially in unmeasured terms and persons prominent in the public eye occasionally flare up at some particularly flagrant manifestation of the itching palm. Governor Whitman, of New York, in an address to the Society for the Prevention of Useless Giving, said (as District Attorney then):

> It is a brave thing, a womanly thing and a courageous thing for you to band together to combat an evil. And I hope you will stand pat. We are all growing to tolerate a kind of petty grafting that is not right, that is un-American. I object to having a man take my hat and hang it up for me and then accept a coin. I am strong and big enough to hang up my own hat. And I also prefer to carry my own bag to having a boy half my size carry a bag that is half his size and be paid with a coin. If he honestly earns the money he should have it as an earning, not as a gratuity. It is this giving of gratuities that is unlike us, it is a custom copied from a foreign country where conditions are different from ours.

Where one person has the courage to speak out against this deep-rooted social convention, unnumbered thousands feel dumbly the same opposition to it. Harry Lauder, the Scotch comedian, a citizen of a monarchy, on one of his tours in America, was reported by the newspapers as being disgusted with the development of so aristocratic a custom as tipping in America, the cradle of democracy. The press will yield many such evidences of condemnation for the practice in high places. They are cited to prove that opposition to tipping is not a mere distaste among persons of limited means who cannot afford to tip generously.

The cost of following the custom is an important item; but those who consider it morally wrong gladly would pay any increase in charges that might follow the abolition of the custom. If the Pullman Company should agree to abolish tipping if each patron would pay a quarter more for his berth it would be a long step in advance—though the custom should be abolished without additional charges to the public.

HUSH MONEY

The United States went through a period of muck-raking against graft among politicians and big business men. It was found that the idea of "honest graft" was shockingly prevalent. The especially odious manifestations were dealt with, but the little springs and rivulets that combine to make the main stream were allowed to trickle along, unite, and become a torrent! Tipping is the training school of graft.

Will a messenger boy who thinks that the public owes him gratuities develop into a man with sound morals? Will the bell-boy who works for tips grow up to be a policeman who accepts hush-money from the corner saloon-keeper? What is the difference between a tip to a bell-boy for doing what the hotel pays him to do and the hush-money to a policeman for overlooking the offence he is paid to detect?

The tipping practice has created an atmosphere of petty graft, the constant breathing of which breeds all other forms of dishonesty. It is small wonder that with so much avarice in low places that we have been shocked by graft in high places. The tipping custom is educating the grafting spirit much faster than the prosecuting arm of the government can destroy it.

There is a direct connection between corruption in elections and the custom of tipping. The man who lives upon tips will not see the dishonesty of selling his vote, so readily as if he discerned the immorality of gratuities. Of course, not all tip-takers sell their votes; but the moral laxity in one direction predisposes toward laxity in other directions.

Splitting Commissions

When a gratuity gets above a small amount, it is known as splitting commissions, or plain graft. Salesmen in their anxiety to sell goods will divide their commissions with the buyers. Frequently buyers or purchasing agents will demand this concession when it has not been offered. One New York department store found that its piano buyer was accepting money for placing all orders with a particular manufacturer. This store discharged its buyer, and yet the proprietor of the store doubtless tipped the waiter at lunch the same day he so acted! He failed to see that a waiter (paid to serve patrons) who accepts tips, is precisely on the same level as a buyer (paid to purchase in the whole market), who concentrates his orders with one house for a fee.

A clipping from *The New York Times* shows the attitude that employers are taking toward split commissions:

> Several wholesalers in this market received a letter yesterday from a prominent dry goods retailer in the middle West saying that their buyers would be in this city to-day and that each one had signified her acceptance of a rule against taking petty 'graft.' The retailer asked that the salesmen try not to make this rule difficult to observe. The rule follows: 'You must not accept entertainment of any kind, even luncheon or dinner, from any one in New York. We will make an allowance, sufficient to cover all expenses, including entertainment.'

This retail merchant had discovered that a free theater ticket or dinner could create such a sense of obligation that his buyers would not be able to exercise the freedom of choice that was necessary. The New York salesmen offered the tickets and dinners in the form of gracious hospitality, but knew all the while that their real intent was to bind the buyers to them through a sense of obligation without regard to the merits of the goods.

Thus the spirit of "honest graft" is spreading out in America. It grows with what it feeds upon. It is a moral miasma, the fumes of which are permeating all strata of society.

The Bible Agaisnt Tips

Following are only a few of the many citations in the Bible against tipping, gifts, gratuities, greed and like practices and impulses:

Exodus 23:8. And thou shalt take no gift; for the gift blindeth the wise, and perverteth the words of the righteous.

Ecclesiastes 7:7. Surely oppression maketh a wise man mad; and a gift destroyeth the heart.

Proverbs 15:27. He that is greedy of gain troubleth his own house; but he that hateth gifts shall live.

I Samuel 12:3. Behold here I am: witness against me before the Lord, and before his anointed: whose ox have I taken? or whose ass have I taken? or whom have I defrauded? whom have I oppressed? or of whose hand have I received any bribe to blind mine eyes therewith? and I will restore it you.

Isaiah 33:14-15. Who among us shall dwell with the devouring fire? . . . He that walketh righteously and speaketh uprightly . . . that shaketh his hands from holding bribes. . . . He shall dwell on high. . . .

Job 15:34. For the congregation of hypocrites shall be desolate, and fire shall consume the tabernacles of bribery.

Luke 12:15. And he said unto them, Take heed and beware of covetousness: for a man's life consisteth not in the abundance of the things which he possesseth.

<h1 style="text-align:center">VII
The Psychology of Tipping</h1>

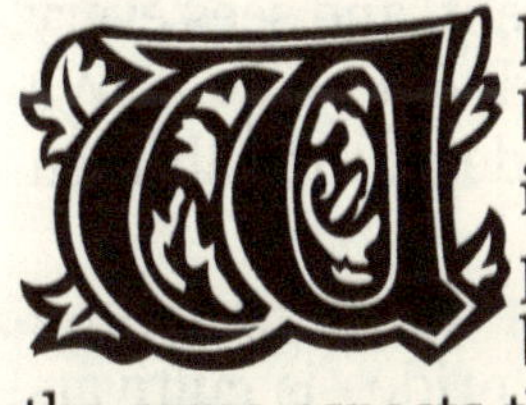 hy the custom of tipping should be followed so generally when it is palpably a bad economic practice and ethically indefensible is a psychological study with the same aspects that the slavery issue presented before the Civil War.

The Puritan conscience allowed that institution to grow to formidable proportions before arousing itself decisively, and it has allowed this equally undemocratic custom to attain national ramifications.

CASTE AND CLASS

In its broadest statement, the psychology of tipping presents the two antipodal qualities of pride
and pusillanimity. The caste system is not based
upon the superiority of one class over another,
but upon the pride that one stage of human development feels over another stage of human development.

A democracy cannot do away with different
stages of development in the human mind. But it
does do away with the belief of one stage of development that it is worthy of homage from another
stage of development. Democracy does not con-
cede that one man working with his brain is superior to another man working with his brawn. Democracy looks beyond the accident of occupation,
or the stage of human development, and sees every
man as originating in the same divine source. "We
hold these truths to be self-evident, that all men
are created equal."

In a monarchy, the craving of the human mind
for approbation—the quality of pride—is cultivated into the class or caste system. Those citizens
who have attained a larger measure of culture than
their fellow-men allow the false sense of pride in
that culture to creep into their ideals and actions.
They seek for some method of visualizing this assumed superiority, of obtaining the acknowledgment of it from their fellow-men. With an unerring
instinct of human nature they play upon the cupid-

ity of those whom they desire to place in a servile relation. A gift of money wins the social distinction they covet.

Thus the tipping custom has its origin in pride, and it necessarily involves humility as a correlative condition. If all men are created equal, as we aver in our basic political creed, they cannot become unequal except artificially, except by an agreement of one set of citizens to play the rôle of servitors for a consideration from another set of citizens. One set of citizens will become abased—that is, they will surrender their birthright of equality—in order that another set may strut around in a belief of superiority and indulge a sense of pride.

No Superior Class

In a democracy, the gradations of culture exist, but it is not permissible for one class of workers to assume a superiority over another class. That they do assume it is evident, and that for all practical social purposes we live and move and have our being on that assumption is evident, but in granting manhood suffrage, in allowing the proud and the humble to have an equal voice in government, we declare the social system a fungus growth.

At the moment of the highest power of the institution of slavery it was not less wrong than at the moment the first ship-load of slaves was landed. No mere accumulation of material property can vitiate a principle of right. Hence, the very widespread acceptance of the tipping custom lends no authority to it. If 95,000,000 Americans are engaged in tipping 5,000,000 Americans, and if both the givers and the receivers apparently concur in the rightness of the custom, it does not thereby become right. We must go back to first principles to find the answer.

TIPPING AND SLAVERY

The American democracy could not live in the face of a lie such as slavery presented, and it cannot live in the face of a lie such as tipping presents. The aim of American statesmanship should be to keep fresh and strong the original concepts of democracy and to beat back the efforts of base human qualities to override these concepts.

The relation of a man giving a tip and a man accepting it is as undemocratic as the relation of master and slave. A citizen in a republic ought to stand shoulder to shoulder with every other citizen, with no thought of cringing, without an assumption of superiority or an acknowledgment of inferiority. This is elementary preaching and yet the distance we have strayed from primary principles makes it necessary to prove the case against tipping.

The psychology of tipping may be stated more in detail in the following formula:

To one-quarter part of generosity add two parts of pride and one part of fear.

FIRST INGREDIENT, GENEROSITY

This is a subtle element and merges into a sense of obligation on slight provocation. You feel that your position in life is more fortunate, and pity enters your thought. If an extra service is given, in reality or in appearance, the servitor has pitched his appeal upon the ground of obligation. Few persons can rest easily until a sense of obligation is discharged through some form of compensation. The opportunity to balance the account comes when cash is being passed between you and the person serving. You offer a cash consideration proportioned to your sense of obligation.

Inasmuch as the whole argument in favor of tipping is based upon the allegation that the servitor actually gives a value in extra service, the element of obligation will be examined closely.

The Pullman porter or the waiter who can succeed in making a patron feel a sense of obligation knows that he has assured a tip for himself. The company or the restaurant business is a vague fact, while the man hovering over your berth or table is a most tangible relation. His art is to make the patron feel that he is responsible for the careful attentions. In a subconscious way the patron knows that the price of the ticket or the food includes the service (wages of the porter or waiter) but the obsequious alertness of the attendant overshadows this knowledge. It is present personality versus an abstract entity known as company or restaurant.

Hence, though the price of the ticket or the payment of the check pays for the porter's or waiter's service, the patron has been made to feel a second obligation which he discharges with a tip.

CLOAKROOM TACTICS

Thus tipping involves two payments for one service. Servitors understand clearly the psychology of the sense of obligation from experiment even though they could not read understandingly a book on psychology. A trial in Detroit over the division of the tips in the cloak-room of a restaurant furnished the following proof:

> 'How do you make people "cough up"?' queried the judge.
>
> 'When they are going away I brush them down, and if they don't give me something I take hold of their lapel and say, "Excuse me," and brush them again. I pretend that's the only English I can speak. If they don't give me something then I hold on to their hats until they do give me something. I made \$12 the first day I worked at the place.'
>
> 'Why did you pretend you could not speak English?' demanded the judge.
>
> 'The more English you know the less tips you get.'

This morally obtuse hat-boy knew that the average person does not want something for nothing when dealing with serving persons, and he exploited this trait to the maximum. Pullman porters and high grade waiters are more polished in the use of the same method, but it all gets back to the idea of creating a sense of obligation by actual or pretended service beyond the expected.

Undoubtedly, a rigid adherence to the letter of duty would result in service that would be unsatisfactory, but this is to be surmounted rightly by the employer requiring flexibility of service from employees—not by the public paying extra for affability, courtesy and attentiveness.

SECOND INGREDIENT, PRIDE

Anxiety to cut a good figure before servants or allied classes of personal workers is a rich vein of pride which they do not fail to work for all it is worth. This kind of mind is always agitated from fear that the tipping has not been done handsomely enough. The satisfaction of having a fellow creature servile before your largess is a factor. The gratuity emphasizes your position in the social scale. It stamps the giver as a gentleman or lady. The smirking attentiveness of the servitor is balm to vanity.

Truly, if it were not for vanity there would be no tipping system.

THIRD INGREDIENT, FEAR

The power behind the tipping custom is Social Convention and the fear of violating it. The so-called social leaders, actuated by aristocratic ideals, establish the custom and the crowd follow suit in a desire to do the "proper" thing. The "what will people say" mania holds the average person in an iron obedience to a custom which is innately loathed. It makes you conspicuous to be a dissenter. The serving persons understand this psychology perfectly. To drift along with the current of social usage is easiest, whereas, to go against it requires the highest order of courage. The multitude simply rate it as one of the petty vices and let it go at that.

THE REMEDY

Now what is the method of meeting and mastering this situation?

Precisely the same reasoning employed by the Americans in 1801 against the custom of paying tribute to the Barbary pirates.

First, establish clearly in your mind that tipping is wrong. The slogan is: ONE COMPENSATION FOR ONE SERVICE. With this premise, you can answer, *seriatim*, every argument which arises in favor of the custom. To the plea of generosity or obligation the reply is, full compensation for all service rendered is included in the bill you pay at the hotel desk, at the ticket window, to the barber-shop cashier, for the taxi-meter reading, and so on. Any extra compensation implied by the person serving is an imposition and has no justification either as charity or obligation.

Second, the promptings of pride must be recognized frankly and mastered by democratic ideals. When a tip is given, not only is an individual wrong done, but a blow is struck at republican government and the ideals upon which it is founded. Patriotism, as well as faithfulness to self-respect requires that all customs which promote class distinctions shall be held in check. In entertaining a democratic attitude toward all Americans you are strengthening the government under which you live. You will not become less of a gentleman or lady if the socially submerged classes rise to a normal plane of self-respect. In declining to place a false valuation upon them you are promoting the true mission of Americanism.

> To thine own self be true,
> And it must follow as the night the day
> Thou canst not then be false to any man.

Third, the fear of violating a social custom is overcome when you understand its pernicious nature. The general observance of it gives the custom neither rightness nor authority. With full assurance that the custom is wrong and with a measure of the courage Decatur showed before Tripoli, an apparently formidable, but really vulnerable, custom can be destroyed.

VIII

The Literature of Tipping

riters of books on etiquette uniformly accept tipping as the correct social usage. They state just the amount that it is proper to give on various occasions and thus do their utmost to rivet the custom upon the people.

A few extracts from such books will be given here to show how the custom is strengthened by the arbiters of etiquette. Those masses of Americans who are aspiring to a broader culture naturally turn to these books, and have their Americanism poisoned at the very start. They are educated to believe that tipping

49

is essential to social grace. The feature departments of newspapers in answering queries about tipping usually confirm this impression, though now and then a side-swipe is delivered at the extortionate attitude of the serving persons.

HOTEL FEES

Taking up the hotel first, the following advice is from *Everyday Etiquette*:[1]

> A porter carries a bag and he must be tipped; another carries up a trunk, he must be tipped; one rings for ice water and the boy bringing it expects his ten cents; one wants hot water every morning and in notifying the chambermaid of this fact, must slip a bit of silver into her palm. The waiter at one's table must be frequently remembered, and the head waiter will give one better attention if he finds something in his hand after he shows the new arrival to a table, and, of course, on leaving one will give a fee.
>
> It is usually best for a transient guest to fee the waiter at each meal, since another man will probably be in attendance at the next one. The usual rate is to give 10 per cent. of the sum paid for the lunch or dinner—ten cents being the minimum except at a restaurant of humble pretensions, where five will be gladly accepted by the waitress.

---

1   Marion Harland and Virginia van de Water, *Everyday Etiquette: A Practical Manual of Social Usages* (Indianapolis: The Bobbs-Merrill Company, 1905). —Ed.

If the waiters and other hotel employees had written the foregoing themselves could they have put it more strongly? Note the advice to tip the waiter at each meal because a new one may be on hand at the next meal! This implies that the failure to tip is a grave offense, and that no risk of giving it must be taken. The patron may rest assured that a new one will be on hand at the next meal, for the head waiter shifts them about for exactly that reason—to make the patron tip again.

However, in this same book, there is a reluctant note, as shown by the following extract:

> We may rebel against the custom and with reason. But as not one of us can alter the state of affairs, it is well to accept it with good grace, or reconcile oneself to indifferent service.

Hotel managers will read this with entire approval. And yet, consider what a contradiction it is for a hotel to advertise its service at such and such rates and then subject its guests to "indifferent service" if they do not cross an itching palm at every angle in the building!

TIP—OR BE INSULTED

Any one who conscientiously objects to tipping knows how true it is that in the "best" places, with one or two notable exceptions, not only "indifferent service" but positively insulting deportment may be expected from the servitors if the tips are omitted.

The servitors are aggressive because their remuneration depends upon what they can work out of the patrons. The employer had hired them on the understanding that any compensation they receive must come from the gratuities of patrons. In certain hotels the management carries the exploitation to the point of charging the servitors for the privilege of working the patrons. The tipping privilege in one hotel has been sold as high as $10,000 a year!

The economic pressure of tipping upon the patron causes one authority on etiquette, *Good Form For All Occasions*,[2] to exclaim:

> Women of frugal mind endeavor to call on these functionaries as little as they can because the cents readily mount into dollars. The elevator-boy receives fewer tips than his peripatetic brother and need not be feed after a short stay.

Here is proof that those who from economic or ethical reasons do not wish to tip are persecuted. They are advised that the easiest way to avoid the displeasure of servitors is to call on them for service as little as possible! The two dollars or more they pay at the hotel desk for a day's domicile must be exclusively for the privilege of sitting in a chair or sleeping in a bed. The moment they require the service of any of the employees about the building,

---

2   Florence Howe Hall, *Good Form for All Occasions* (New York and London: Harper & Brothers Publishers, 1914). —Ed.

they are under a second obligation to pay. And yet, hotels prate about their "hospitality." The Barbary pirates were hospitable in the same way—after you paid the tribute!

HOW THE BOOKS HELP

The Cyclopædia of Social Usage[3] states the tipping obligation as follows:

> In a large and fashionable hotel generous and widely diffused gratuities are expected by the employees. The experienced traveler usually distributes in gratuities a sum equal to ten per cent. of the amount of the bill. It is customary when a lengthy sojourn is made in an hotel or pension to tip the chambermaid, the various waiters and the porter who does one's boots, once in every week. Once in every fortnight the head waiter's expectations should be satisfied, and where an elevator boy and doorman are on duty, they, too, have claims on the purse of the guest.
>
> In a fashionable European hotel the rule of tipping a franc a week all around may safely be observed during a long stop. But at the hour of departure something extra must be added to the weekly franc, and the head waiter will scarcely smile as blandly as need be if he is not propitiated with gold.

Others, the writer says, have claims that it is well to recognize and meet before they urge them.

---

3   Helen Lefferts Roberts, *The Cyclopaedia of Social Usage* (New York: G.P. Putnam's Sons, 1913). —Ed.

Practically all the books on etiquette have the same note of subserviency to the custom. The point to be remembered is that, without being conscious of it, these writers are in league with the beneficiaries of the custom to perpetuate and extend it. Most of the authors think the custom is right, they have the aristocratic viewpoint that servants should "know their place" and, in a republic, be made to acknowledge it by accepting a gratuity. Others simply take conditions as they find them and write to inform readers how to avoid unpleasant incidents. But regardless of the opinion of the writers on the ethics of the custom, the books are one of the principal supports of the custom.

Leaving the hotel, and considering the tipping custom in its relation to private hospitality, we find this advice in *Dame Curtesy's Book of Etiquette*:[4]

> It is customary to give servants a tip when one remains several days under a friend's roof. The sum cannot be stated but common sense will settle the question.

IN PRIVATE HOUSES

The theory of tipping to servants in private homes where one may be a guest is based on the assumption that one's presence gives the servants extra work and they should be compensated therefor.

---

4   Ellye Howell Glover, *Dame Curtsey's Book of Etiquette* (Chicago: A. C. McClurg, 1909). —Ed.

The extra work undoubtedly is involved, but in a really true conception of hospitality, should not the servants enter into it as much as the hosts? Or, if the guest entails extra work should not the host's conception of hospitality cause him or her to supply the extra compensation? The guest who tips servants in a private home implies that the host or hostess has not adequately compensated them for their labor.

The tips under such circumstances are a reflection upon the hospitality of the home. A host should ascertain if servants consider themselves outside the feeling of hospitality and pay them for the extra work, thus giving the guest complete hospitality. It is bad enough to tip in a hotel, for professional hospitality; to tip in a private home is, or should be, an insult to the host.

ON OCEAN VOYAGES

The same author advises in regard to the Pullman car that "a porter should receive a tip at the end of the journey, large or small according to the length of the trip and the service rendered," and then considers the custom aboard a ship, as follows:

> There is much tipping to be done aboard a ship. Two dollars all around is a tariff fixed for persons of average means, and this is increased to individual servants from whom extra service has been demanded.

The traveler boards a ship with a ticket of passage which includes stateroom and meals and all service requisite to the proper enjoyment of these privileges. The stewards and other employees on board are expressly for the purpose of giving the service the ticket promised. Hence, extra compensation to them may be justified only as charity. They cannot possibly render extra service for which they should be paid. If a passenger called upon the engineer to render a service, that employee would be rendering an extra service, but stewards and stewardesses and like employees are aboard to render any service the passenger wants or needs. Moving deck chairs, bringing books, attending to calls to your stateroom, serving you food and the like duties are all within the scope of their regular employment.

But read another writer's pronouncement:

> At the end of an ocean voyage of at least five days' duration, the fixed tariff of fees exacts a sum of two dollars and a half per passenger to every one of those steamer servants who have ministered daily to the traveler's comfort.
>
> Thus single women would give this sum to the stewardess, the table steward, the stateroom steward, and, if the stewardess has not prepared her bath, she bestows a similar gratuity on her bath steward. If every day she has occupied her deck chair, he also will expect two dollars and fifty cents.
>
> Steamers there are on which the deck boys must be remembered with a dollar each, and

> where a collection is taken up, by the boy who polishes the shoes and by the musicians.
>
> On huge liners patronized by rich folks exclusively, the tendency is to fix the minimum gratuity at $5, with an advance to seven, ten and twelve where the stewardess, table steward and stateroom steward are concerned."

Then follow instructions to tip the smoking-room steward, the barbers and even the ship's doctor!

THE "RICH AMERICANS" MYTH

It is small wonder, in view of the nature of the literature of tipping, that Europe has found American travelers "rich picking." Before embarking on the first trip abroad the average American informs himself and herself of what is expected in the way of gratuities, and everywhere the tourist turns in a library advice is found which effectually throws the cost of service upon the patron. Railroad and steamship literature usually avoids the subject because these companies do not want to bring this additional expense of travel to the attention of the public. A steamship folder will state that passage to London is ninety dollars, including berth and meals, but gives no hint that the tips will amount to ten dollars more!

IX
Tipping and the Stage

An almost invariable laugh-producer on the stage or in moving pictures is a scene in which a bell-boy or other servitor executes the customary maneuvers for obtaining a tip. Play producers know that the laugh can be evoked and any hotel scene is certain to include this bit of business. In seeking the explanation of the humor in such a scene, the answer will be found to be cynicism and the peculiar glee that people feel in observing others in disagreeable situations.

COMIC WOES

The slap-stick variety of comedy is based upon this trait in human nature. If a man is kicked down three flights of stairs, the spectator howls with delight. And, particularly, if a policeman is worsted in an encounter, the merriment is frenzied. Our Sunday comic papers depend almost exclusively upon violence for their humor. It is the final spanking the Katzenjammer Kids receive that brings the laugh. The climax to many other comics—notably *Mutt and Jeff*—is violence.

Hence, a tipping scene on the stage or in moving pictures creates a laugh because the public sees the tip-giver as a victim. He usually exaggerates his rôle by making the giving of the tip a painful act to himself, and the whole scene proves the contention in this discussion, namely, that tipping is wrong. If the spectators did not perceive the bell-boy as a bandit, and the hotel guest as a victim, no laugh would result. They have been in similar situations and know the feelings of the victim.

Sometimes stage managers vary the incident so that the laugh is on the bell-boy, by having the guest refrain from tipping. Then the spectators laugh at the bell-boy's disappointment—again finding humor in misfortune.

TIPS IN THE MOVIES

With the development of moving pictures the utilization of this kind of humor has widened immeasurably. And the point to be considered here is the influence of such visualization of tipping upon the spread of the custom. Undoubtedly tipping is increased by moving pictures and by stage representation. The public is made to feel that, despite the inherent wrong in the custom, it must be followed, or they will experience the unpleasantness at which they have just laughed.

Another example of the itching palm which may be depended upon to produce a laugh is a scene in which a policeman is handed a bill for neglecting his duty in some respect. A well-to-do man will cross the law in some manner and in the play he winks an eye, the policeman turns his back with his palm extended, a bill is slipped into it, and he departs to the sound of the spectators' laugh.

The effect of these scenes upon the public is dual. It either confirms their impression that all servants or officers are "approachable," or it creates among the unsophisticated the idea that tipping or graft is the customary and proper method of dealing with such classes of citizens. The worldly wise gain the first impression, and the spread of the tipping custom is assured by the second impression.

Moving pictures have extended this influence to every nook and corner of the country. The result is that persons who live in the smaller and more democratic communities are educated to the big city development of the itching palm. And the effect upon children and young people is pernicious in the extreme.

IMPRESSING THE YOUNG

A boy who sees a tipping scene in a moving picture gains the impression that it is smart to exact such tribute. Or he gains the impression that he has been overlooking a rich vein of easy remuneration. The photo-play directors, either consciously or unconsciously, are doing great damage to democratic ideals by featuring such scenes. It will not be surprising if, among the other evils fostered by moving pictures, the next generation displays a marked increase in the grafting propensity. The young people are being educated to think it natural.

Thus, aside from the human impulses of pride and avarice, it is apparent that literature and the stage are strengthening the custom of tipping by their representations of it as humorous. People will not combat anything at which they laugh. The itching palm has two doughty champions in the books on etiquette and the theaters.

Actors, it would seem, have enough contact with the itching palm among stage hands to make them ardent advocates of reform, to say nothing of their contact with it in hotels. On the vaudeville stage especially the carpenter, the electrician, the property man and their co-workers must be "seen" with regular and generous donations to insure a smooth act. In many theaters the stage hands have a definite scale of tips for regular duties that they perform—and for which the management also pays them.

X

The Employee Viewpoint

rom a waiter, or a porter, or a janitor's point of view, tipping is wrong only when it is meager. They regard this form of compensation as not only just but usually too sparingly bestowed.

Unquestionably, with any reform in the manner of compensation to persons engaged in domestic or other serving capacities, must go a reform in the attitude of the public toward servitors. The patron who abuses his privileges, who exacts of employees far more than he has the right to ask, who treats them as automatons without sensibilities or self-respect—such a patron must be handled simultaneously with the change in manner of compensation.

Employers, particularly in hotels and like public places, will have to give more attention to seeing that employees are not mistreated by the swaggering, blatant, selfish type of patron. This type abounds and has been developed largely by the tipping custom, that is, the extremely servile attitude assumed by servitors in order to stimulate tipping has brought out the opposite quality of domineering pride in the patron.

THE SORE SPOT

No feeling so rankles in the mind as the sense of uncompensated labor. The thought that patrons have gotten something for nothing leaves a sore spot in the thought of servitors. And if they are employed in places where the only compensation they receive is from the gratuities of patrons, this soreness is incurable. The next time the patron appears he will be made to feel the displeasure of the employee. Thus, in one sense, it is the system that is wrong, a system which does an injustice to both employee and patron.

Every employee has a fairly clear idea of his duties. Most employees scrupulously refrain from doing more than the duties for which they are paid expressly. Hence, when an employee over-steps this boundary he has fixed in his own mind, he has the sense of uncompensated labor. He feels a grudge either against the employer or the patron. He looks to one or the other to supply the extra remuneration for the extra service.

As a consequence, personal service workers are nursing a grievance much of the time. Their conversation and thoughts are about some patron who has failed to compensate them, or has, in their judgment, inadequately compensated them. They devote little time to thinking of a reform in the system that would give them an adequate compensation from the employer and do away entirely with the patron-to-employee form of compensation.

THE MARTYR

The tipping system is so established now that the individual who opposes it must be prepared to play the rôle of martyr, whether employee or patron. Employers who profit by the no-wage system dislike employees with a degree of self-respect that makes them rebel at gratuities. Such wages as are paid are so nominal that the employee cannot subsist upon them alone. He either has to quit that line of work or enter it and conform to the conventional methods.

In Chapter V the equity of tipping certain employees was considered and the claim of other employees as to their rights will be considered briefly here.

BAGGAGEMEN

Tipping men who call for and deliver trunks has become a fixed custom in the cities and is expected, though not so often practiced, in the smaller towns. The transfer company theoretically charge for the complete operation of moving the trunk from the home or hotel to the railroad station. But the men on the wagons or trucks exact tips for carrying the baggage up and down stairs or elevators. The question is, are they entitled to this extra compensation? The baggagemen argue that their business, strictly interpreted, is to carry the trunk from the house to the station and that going up stairs and into rooms is an extra service. Hence, they stand around and make it evident that they expect compensation from the patron, in addition to their wages from the company.

Their position is not tenable. A patron pays the company to get his trunk from wherever it may be and to deliver it to its destination. Whatever operations are necessary to get the trunk are the natural duties of the company and its employees. The charges of the company are, or should be, based on the complete service. The exaction of extra compensation in the form of tips by the employees, therefore, is an imposition. In calling the company no person, tacitly or openly, agrees to the argument that the trunk is to be moved from curb to curb.

The understanding is that your baggage is to be removed from its customary place in the home to the customary place in the station or other destination. It would be as reasonable for baggagemen to dump a trunk outside a station and demand a gratuity from the railroad for bringing it inside, as to demand a gratuity from the patron for taking the trunk up or down stairs. Tipping to baggagemen is unnecessary. If the company pays inadequate wages the remedy lies not from the patron through tips but from the employer through the payment of increased wages.

BOOTBLACKS

Of late years the custom has grown up to tip bootblacks. This is in addition to the regular charge paid for the service and has no justification except in the false plea of the servitor that if the patron does not tip him he will have no compensation. Here it may be stated that the thought that the tip constitutes the only compensation the employee receives is the chief influence in the mind of the patron. He feels a pity for the employee even though he objects to the bad economic system that enables employers to engage workers on such a basis. The employees exploit this thought in the mind by leading the conversation with the patron into the channel of compensation. At some time during the service he lets the patron know that the tips he receives are his only compensation and this arouses the sense of obligation in the patron who does not like to have his shoes shined for nothing, even though the payment at the desk covers the transaction.

Any one who has patronized a restaurant regularly, or a bootblack stand, or a barbershop, or manicurist, or any public place, will recall how invariably the servitors bring up the subject of tipping and always with the suggestion that they would be disabled financially if it were not for the generosity of the public.

This is all a carefully and skilfully planned campaign to exploit the patron.

BARBER SHOP PORTERS

Patrons who do not tip barbers frequently tip the porters who brush them down. On the surface it seems that the porter's attentions in a barber shop are extra and deserve extra compensation. Yet, theoretically, no master barber would admit that a patron of his shop has any other charges to pay than the regular tariffs. The porter is there as an extra measure of service from the shop. Practically, however, the shops all proceed on the assumption of tipping. The porter is a much-aggrieved individual if he is overlooked. In any sound economic system, the porter's compensation should come exclusively from the shop. If his attentions are decided to be extra, there should be a regular scale of compensation, as for a hair cut, which the patron should pay. So long as his services are furnished by the shop without being included in the regular shop tariffs, the patron owes the porter nothing for his attentions.

The solution of the whole tipping problem lies in the foregoing postulate—that if any employee is in a position to render an extra service there should be a regular scale of charges for such service. It is the irregular compensation, depending upon the whim of the patron, that makes the practice economically unsound. No hotel, or other employer, should have on the premises any employee whose compensation depends upon chance. If a hotel stations an employee in the washroom he should be there distinctly as part of the service for which a patron pays at the cashier's desk. A porter in a barber shop should be engaged exclusively at the shop's expense as part of the complete service for which a patron pays to the cashier. Employers, however, are much too shrewd to scatter employees around on the formal understanding that the patrons are to compensate them. They pretend that they are engaged as an extra measure of courtesy or service from the employer and then are educated to exact, through tips, their compensation from the patron.

Door Men

It would seem that if there were any place where the patron might feel free to forget his coin pocket, it would be in the use of doors. But it is customary now to tip door men. That is, you have to pay to enter a hotel, a restaurant or other public place in order to spend money with the employer. The employer will smile blandly and assure you that no patron need tip the door man, but the door man will give unmistakable evidence to the contrary. The tipping of door men shows how the custom grows with what it feeds upon. To the devotee of the custom every underling has an itching palm that must be scratched with a coin and the employer rejoices because it relieves him of wage-payments. Tipping doormen is incomprehensibly weak. Elevator men are in the same class.

GUIDES

In parks and other public places where the employer or the Government furnishes guides and where patrons pay a regular fee for being shown the sights, the guides carefully cultivate the tipping propensity. Their most common method is to start a conversation about how inadequately they are paid for their work and the high cost of living. They play upon the sympathies of the sight-seers until at the end of the trip the feeling is strong that the guide should be remembered. He pockets the gratuity and looks for other game. The patrons overlook the fact that if he is underpaid the employer or the Government is at fault. He often works in the appearance of extra attentions to create the sense of obligation. It is clearly a case of double compensation for one service.

HAT-BOYS

The cloak-room is one of the best devices for throwing the item of wages to the shoulders of patrons. For some one to check and guard your hat and overcoat while you see a show or dine has a speaking likeness to a real extra service. But it is as counterfeit as the other pretenses of extra service. It is every restaurant's or theater's duty to provide for hats and coats of patrons. The meal or the show cannot be enjoyed unless this preliminary function is performed by the proprietor. When two dollars is paid for a theater ticket it also pays for this service, and extra compensation to the attendant in charge may be defended as charity but not as an obligation. A patron who buys a meal in a restaurant owes the cloak-room attendants nothing. He paid for their service in paying for the meal. Tips to hat-boys are superfluous.

JANITORS

The autocrat of the basement is a man with a grievance even when generously tipped. From his viewpoint he is called upon to do a score of things outside his duties. Must he do these for nothing? He must not. The only question is who shall pay him. The janitor should be hired by employers upon the understanding that the renters have the right of way in utilizing his services. Or, apartments should be leased with a clear understanding of the janitor's duties, so that he will have no lee-way to exploit the renters. On the face of it, the idea of defining a janitor's services so that everything outside of the regulations would be extra service for which the renter should compensate him, seems difficult of execution. But the difficulty is less real than apparent. And in the meantime, the janitor regularly is tipped to do things for which he is paid by the employer. He is "out for his" as eagerly as the waiter or the Pullman porter. Hallboys in the apartment houses are equally avaricious. Now and then the metropolitan papers contain letters to the editor complaining of their exactions—pathetic letters from well-to-do persons paying thousands of dollars' rent for apartments! One way out would be to insert in a lease that the renter shall receive full and equal service without extra compensation to employees.

MANICURISTS

These young women have the best psychological opportunity to exact tribute, particularly where the patrons are men. The personal contact is influential, and the plaintive tale of meager salary and small tips which she purrs into your ears, the meanwhile flashing a languishing smile—it's a great little game which she plays for all it is worth! Some of them receive eight dollars a week in "salary," and the tips amount to enough to make their income thirty-five a week and more. The employer has the fifty, seventy-five cents or a dollar charge for the service as practically clear profit. Many men tip the manicurist as much as they pay for the service. Perhaps many of them feel that they get their money's worth in social enjoyment—not believing that the young woman bestows the same charm upon every other male victim! "I feel sorry for that little Miss Brown. If it wasn't for the tips she couldn't live on her salary," said one sympathetic man. He objected to tipping as a rule, but here was a clear case where it was worthy! No use arguing ethics with him.

MESSENGERS

The custom of pay to telegraph messenger boys by the recipients of messages is peculiarly reprehensible because it is fixing a standard of graft in his mind that will work out into worse practices in maturity. A boy given a tip has had his self-respect punctured in a dangerous way. He may grow up and out of such a conception of compensation, but it will be a struggle, and much of our police and other public graft had its origin in the cultivation of the belief that "tips" are proper. A messenger boy has absolutely no claim upon a patron for extra compensation. The price of a telegram includes the cost of delivery.

STENOGRAPHERS

Public typists often expect gratuities. The regular charges are for "the house." They want something for themselves on the side. Sometimes the tips are so large that the employer gets greedy and requires them to be turned in, as proved by the following extract from a want ad in *The New York Times*:

> Remuneration half of all you make with weekly guarantee of $20; proceeds net more than guarantee. No smoking; tips must be turned in.

It seems self-evident that anything given to stenographers beyond the regular charges for the work is pure waste. They cannot possibly give any service in return, and cannot retain the proper self-respect in accepting something for nothing. Many of them, however, take the tips simply to avoid offending patrons.

The list of tip-takers is too extensive for individual consideration. Bath attendants, bartenders, house servants, clerks—and so on through a lamentably long list, have the same moral disease. The contagion is spreading in an alarming way. Of course, the whole system is riding for a fall.

The spurious and specious arguments of employees in behalf of the custom and the timorous acquiescence of the public will alike yield before a robust and elemental Americanism.

XI
The Employer Viewpoint

"e face a condition, not a theory," assert those employers who defend their adaptation of wages to the tipping custom. "The public seems determined to bestow gratuities, and if we paid full wages in addition, our employees would be the highest paid workers in the world."

But two wrongs do not make a right.

THREE KINDS OF EMPLOYERS

Employers who profit by tipping are classified as follows:

77

1. Those who pay living wages and positively forbid gratuities.

2. Those who pay average competitive wages and maintain a passive attitude toward gratuities.

3. Those who pay minimum, or no, wages, and aggressively exploit the propensity to give.

At present the first class constitutes almost an infinitesimal minority. Here and there in large cities there are barber shops which advertise a "No-Tip" policy, and occasionally a hotel or restaurant.

In the second class are most of the moderate-price places catering to the public. The employers and employees welcome gratuities but do not make them the prime object in their relations with patrons.

The third class includes the high-grade hotels, sleeping car companies, expensively conducted restaurants and like enterprises. This is the class which sets the pace through the patronage of the socially or financially prominent.

A few of the more noteworthy employers who profit by the custom follow:

The Pullman Company,
The Hotel Company,
The Taxicab Company,
The Transfer Company,
The Steam Ship Company,
The Master Barber,
The Apartment House Owner,

The Restaurant,
The Telegraph Company.

That an organized conspiracy exists between employers and employees to exploit the public is realized vaguely, if at all, by the average patron.

Proof of this allegation may be found at the cashier's desk of almost any restaurant or hotel. The waiter invariably is given change that will make it easy for the patron to tip. He returns with the change arranged in such a way on the tray that the patron must fumble over all of it if he wants the full amount. The employer's and the waiter's theory is that, rather than do this, he will leave a dime or a quarter in one corner. In a barber shop the patron always receives small change so that it will be easy to "remember" the porter.

Yet, such a practice is the mildest indictment that may be brought against employers for entering a conspiracy to exploit patrons.

SELLING THE TIP PRIVILEGE

In New York and Chicago particularly, many employers went so far (and still maintain the practice) as to sell to outside persons and companies the privilege of collecting the tips in their places of business. That is to say, these outside parties were to furnish waiters, cloak room attendants and other employees to the hotel or restaurant and depend upon the tips for their remuneration.

So large was the sum realized from tips that the hotels and restaurants actually charged the outside parties thousands of dollars for the concession. In Illinois a law was passed in 1915 aimed directly at this organized phase of the custom. It prohibited hotels and others from selling tipping privileges. The men who owned such privileges promptly went to law to test the constitutionality of the act. To the tip-taker anything is unconstitutional that interferes with his graft!

At the time the law went into effect, the situation was reported in *The Chicago Tribune* as follows:

> The state will have a fight on its hands before the Chicago tip trust . . . releases its clutch on the pocketbooks of hotel and restaurant patrons.
>
> At midnight last night . . . there was no indication the largess was going anywhere else than it has gone before ever since a commercial genius capitalized the well-known generosity of the dining and wining public—straight into the coffers of the trust.

The manager of one of the leading hotels said that lawyers for the hotel had served notice on the head of the biggest of Chicago's three tip trusts to withdraw his minions.

> "Do you contemplate returning part of the money paid for the concession?" he was asked.
>
> "That," the manager replied, "is a detail."
>
> "Do you think it possible (the head of the tip

trust) will resist expulsion?"

"Hardly. We'll just put in a crew of our own and that will end it."

"Have you heard a report that the tip trusts contemplate standing by their guns and, if necessary, charging a 10 cent fee for checking hats and coats, anticipating the tip?"

"That's preposterous."

After such evidence, patrons of hotels and other public service places hardly will feel as cheerful in giving tips as they may have felt before being enlightened. Here was a typical instance of a hotel advertising such and such rates for rooms and food with the plain inference that patrons had no other obligation. Then the management goes out and sells the right to exploit the patrons, thereby filling its dining rooms and cloak rooms with employees who must exact tips if they are to be paid at all for their work!

ARE YOU A BENEFACTOR?

A small part of the public cares nothing about this and will tip regardless of the conditions of employment of the servitors. This element simply enjoys the grandiloquent rôle of Bestower of Largess. But the vast majority of Americans has followed the custom under duress. This majority finds it repugnant to tip on the assumption that the employee alone profits by its generosity; and to discover that the employer as well profits by it—in fact secretly devises methods of encouraging the tipping—will confirm the majority in the thought that the custom is wholly bad.

Under which school of economics, or ethics, can such a system be justified?

The assertion of employers that tipping is the spontaneous impulse of patrons and that they cannot afford to pay living wages in addition is seen to be without foundation in conspicuous instances. Such spontaneity as exists they stimulate and exploit for their own profit.

Conceding that the development of tipping has thrown employment upon an abnormal basis, the question arises, if tipping is abolished should the increase in wages be borne exclusively by the employer?

To the extent that employers make extraordinary dividends out of the custom the extra cost of operation through normal wages should be borne by them without increased tariffs to patrons. Competition in the hotel business, for example, has been adjusted to the custom of tipping and the sudden throwing of a bona fide wage system upon such employers, without an increase in revenues, would be disastrous.

A Reasonable Solution

The solution in certain instances might be found in a joint obligation of patron and employer. The employer says: "I have been able to give you food at such and such a price because I have not had to charge to it the cost of waiter hire. If the public discontinues gratuities to my employees, I must raise the price of food to cover this deficit." The patron replies: "Upon proof that your food tariffs have not included the item of waiter-hire, I will pay more for my meals if they are served free."

The goal of a reform in tipping is to make one payment—and that one to the employer—cover every expense of the patron.

Even if the public should have to pay more for food, lodging and other service, if tipping is abolished, an immense advance in sound economics and democratic ethics would be made in eliminating the double-payment system. Where two payments are made—to employer and employee—it is inevitable that the patron will lose.

It should be understood, however, that a large part of the $200,000,000 or more given annually by Americans in gratuities is sheer waste because it is given for absolutely nothing in return. Such waste should be eliminated without consideration of employer or employee.

So long as employers assume that the public will pay part or all of the wages of employees, so long will the employees be under the necessity of resorting to outrageous tactics—coddling the patron who does tip, insulting and neglecting the one who does not tip—in order to obtain pay for their services.

Employers must come to the viewpoint that tipping is morally wrong, and therefore of necessity, economically unsound. The money they make out of tipping is tainted money. Employees should be engaged on wages that are adequate without regard to any gratuities that may be given.

XII

One Step Forward

 hen the Hotel Statler, in Buffalo, announced that a guest need not tip its employees in order to get satisfactory service, a sensation was sprung upon hotel managers and the traveling public. Nothing more emphatically shows the abnormal state of mind toward tipping than that such an elementary right should be affirmed and cause surprise in the affirmation.

A Sound Code

Following is its Code to employes on the practice

85

of tipping:

The patron of a hotel goes there because he expects to receive certain things served with celerity, courtesy and cheerfulness.

The persons who are to fetch and carry him these things will be those whose portion it is to render intimate, personal services to others. Since time immemorial, this class of servitors has been of the rank and file.

Now and then a server is found—a waiter, a bootblack, a barber or a bell boy—who adds a bit of his own personality to his services. Such a one shows a bit more intelligence—initiative—perspicacity—than his fellows. The patron finds his smaller wants anticipated, and is pleased. He feels that the servant has given him something extra and unexpected—and he wants to pay something extra for it.

He tips.

Of course there are abuses of the tip. A rich bounder wants something more than other hotel guests, and he futilely tries to get it by throwing money about.

His tips are insults, and his reward Servility instead of service.

Or—

An individual wishing to be thought a 'good fellow' ADMINISTERS tips with the advice to 'buy a house and lot,' etc.

Or—

An infrequent traveler, having the time of his life, tips out of sheer goodheartedness.

These types help to constitute the 'Public.'

It is the business of a good hotel to cater to the Public. It is the avowed business of the Hotel

Statler to please the public better than any other hotel in the world.

Statler can run a tipless hotel if he wants to.

But Statler knows that a first-class hotel cannot be maintained on a tipless basis, for the reason that a small but certain per cent. of its guests will tip, in spite of all rules.

Statler can and does do this: He guarantees to his guests who do not wish to tip, everything—EVERYTHING—in the way of hotel service, courtesy, etc., that the tipper gets.

Let's make that a bit stronger—guests do NOT have to tip at Hotel Statler to get courteous, polite, attentive service.

Or, for final emphasis, we say to Statler guests: Please do NOT tip unless you feel like it; but if you DO tip, let your tipping be yielding to a genuine desire—not conforming to an outrageous custom.

Any Statler employee who is wise and discreet enough to merit tips is wise and discreet enough to render a like service whether he is tipped or not.

And he is wise and discreet enough to say 'thank you' when he gets his tip.

In this connection let this be said:

The man who takes a tip and does not thank the tipper does not feel that he has earned the tip any more than a blackmailer feels that he has earned his blood money.

Any Statler employee who fails to give Service, or who fails to thank the guest who gives him something, falls short of the Statler Standard. We always thank any guest who reports such a case to us. Statler does not deal summarily with his helpers, any more than he deals perfunctori-

ly with his guests—but the tip-grafters get short
shrift here."

FOR THE BENEFIT OF GUESTS

To understand the spirit of management which
could issue such instructions to its employees in the
face of the opportunity to exploit the public, as most
hotels do and so throw the whole cost of wages upon
the patron, it is necessary to consider other sections
of the Code treating of professional hospitality.

> Hotel Statler is operated primarily for the
> benefit and convenience of its guests. Without
> guests there could be no Hotel Statler. These
> are simple Facts easily understood.
> The Statler is a successful hotel. The Reason
> is, that every Waiter in this hotel, every Hall-
> Boy, the Chambermaid, the Clerk, the Chef, the
> Manager, the Boss Himself, is working all the
> time to make them FEEL 'at home.'
> Hotel service—that is, Hotel Statler service—
> means the limit of Courteous, Efficient Atten-
> tion from Each Particular Employee to Each
> Particular Guest. This is the kind of service a
> Guest pays for when he pays us his bill—wheth-
> er it is for $2.00 or $20.00 per day. It is the
> kind of Service he is entitled to, and he NEED
> NOT and SHOULD NOT pay ANY MORE.

NOT HOSPITALITY

Compare the attitude of management toward
guests as revealed in this code with the bristling,

belligerent attitude of employees in other first-class places where tipping is undisciplined! In the average hotel where the management encourages the tipping for economic reasons the bell-boy will make a scene if you fail to tip him after he carries your suit-case from the lobby to your room. Every other employee has the same spirit—he has to have it if he is to be compensated at all, for the employer puts it squarely up to him to work the guest for his wages.

Apparently this hotel reached the conviction that this was not hospitality.

Then the conviction was reached that a guest "need not and should not pay any more" for hotel service than the rate paid at the desk. From this it was logical to bring the employees to a new conception of service and to stop the piratical practice toward guests who do not tip.

It is particularly significant to note the assertion that the proprietor can run a tipless hotel if he wants to. That is an interesting declaration. It proves that those managers who exploit the tipping propensity deliberately do so for reasons of greed.

Then the reason for not running a tipless hotel is stated to be that "a small but certain per cent. of its guests will tip in spite of all rules." Here is evidence that the public has its measure of blame for the custom as well as the avarice of managers. This hotel declares that its conception of hospitality is to leave the guest free in his relation toward employees. But note this! *It does not leave the employees free in their attitude toward guests.*

UP TO THE EMPLOYER

The foregoing distinction is the crux of the whole tipping problem. If managers will restrain and discipline employees so that they will not run riot in their eagerness to exact toll from patrons the tipping evil will be reduced to a minimum.

THE FIRST STEP

It is not the idea underlying this discussion to consider that a satisfactory disposal of the tipping custom has been made when managers insure equal treatment for those who do not tip in comparison with those who do tip. Nothing short of the complete abolition of the custom can be the goal in a republic. But as a long stride toward the goal, the Code cited above is noteworthy. It constitutes the first immediate step that any hotel may take.

The public would find immense relief in the general adoption of the foregoing idea—that tipping must "be yielding to a genuine desire—not conforming to an outrageous custom." Inasmuch as the vast majority of Americans who tip do so only because they are afraid not to conform to an outrageous custom, this plan, honestly enforced upon employees, will reduce the followers of the custom to the small percentage of the public who tip because of pride or moral obtuseness. A way can be found to handle this element when the majority have been freed.

Once the proof is at hand that tipping can be handled the conclusion is unescapable that the managers who knuckle to the custom are "corrupt and contented." They are on precisely the same moral level as their employees.

The Guest's Rights

In the meantime, the individual patron has the right to and should proceed on the theory that he is entitled to EVERYTHING in the way of service for the one payment. This is his common law right even if no special laws regulating tipping are in force.

The public is at a great disadvantage in combating the tipping evil when the managers leave the issue to be settled between the patrons and the employees. A bell boy can commit an offense to a patron who does not tip that is perfectly tangible to the patron but difficult to report to the manager. Unless the manager takes a positive hand and instructs his employees in a manner similar to the above Code it is likely that most persons will continue to pay tribute rather than be insulted and neglected.

In Chicago, the Young Men's Christian Association operates a nineteen-story hotel where tips are prohibited, and this organization generally discourages the custom in its enterprises.

XIII

The Sleeping-Car Phase

he Pullman Company stands in the public mind as the leading exponent of tipping. It certainly is the largest beneficiary of the custom, as a simple calculation will show.

The company has about 6,500 porters, who receive $27.50 a month in wages. Suppose the porters received no tips. The company then would have to pay living wages. Assuming that the long hours of work would not attract desirable porters under a straight wage system without at least $60 a month pay, each one of the 6,500 would have an increase of $32.50 a month, or $390 a year.

This would mean an increase in the company's annual pay-roll of $2,535,000!

In other words, the company saves about two and a half millions a year through the tips given to its porters. What part of the large annual dividend is furnished by this saving is a secret of the company's books.

Some of these porters after many years' service receive $42 a month in wages, and this would bring down the foregoing estimate, though not to any radical extent. The tips bring their incomes to $100, $150, $200 and more a month! There are, of course, many runs on which the porters derive smaller amounts in gratuities, and the best runs are given as a reward for long and faithful service.

WHAT THE PULLMAN MANAGER SAID

The Walsh Commission,[1] appointed to investigate industrial conditions in the United States, in 1915 singled out the Pullman tipping practice for investigation. Some of the testimony given by the general manager of the company follows:

> "The company simply accepts conditions as it finds them. The company did not invent tipping. It was here when the company began."

---

[1] Also known as the Commission on Industrial Relations, it was created by the U.S. Congress on August 23, 1912, to scrutinise U.S. labor law. The commission studied work conditions throughout the industrial United States between 1913 and 1915, and published its eleven-volume final report in 1916. —Ed.

"What do you say to making tipping unlawful and paying employees a living wage?" Chairman Walsh asked.

"If such a condition arises, I presume we would have to pay wages necessary to get the service."

"Do you get your negroes in the South?"

"Yes, we have been looking after them in the South. The South is a bigger field and the men there are more adapted for the work than the Northern negroes."

"Well, be plain," Chairman Walsh said, "are the negroes from the South more docile and less independent than those from the North?"

"Well, no, but the Southern negro is more pleasing to the traveling public. He is more adapted to wait on people and serve with a smile."

"Can a man live on $27.50 a month and rear a family?"

"Really, I don't know. He might."

"Does the Pullman Company have in mind the liberality and kindness of the public when it fixes that rate of pay?"

"Well, I should say that tips have something to do with it. I didn't make the rates of pay."

"A porter must call passengers during the night, polish shoes, answer bells, and look after the safety and comfort of the passengers at all hours, must he not?"

"Yes. He is reprimanded, suspended or discharged for infractions of the rules."

"What is your attitude toward the question of an organization among your employees?"

"I felt that the movement to form a federation of our employees was a selfish one on the part of a few."

WHAT THE PORTERS SAID

The Commission also called several porters to testify. They stated that they could not live without the tips. One porter with twenty-one years' service behind him testified that he receives $42 a month in wages, while the tips averaged about $75 a month, or $117 income from the company and the public.

Another porter receiving $27.50 a month testified that his tips averaged about $77 a month. He was described as wearing two diamond rings and being tastefully dressed.

The conductors receive from $70 to $90 a month in salary, and it was brought out before the Commission that many do not consider it dishonest to "knock down" on seat sales. This is accomplished partly at the company's expense, and partly at the expense of patrons—especially unsophisticated travelers who buy a whole seat but have other passengers sit beside them, the conductor pocketing the extra payment. This practice is limited to day runs. There is also the opportunity to overcharge.

That the Pullman Company gives the public good service through its porters is indisputable. The only question is whether the public should pay extra for this service. If a porter with an income of $117, say, receives only $27.50 from the company, the public is paying three-fourths of his wages and the company only one-fourth. Where the porters have incomes of $150 to $200 a month the company pays one-fifth to one-eighth of the amount and the public pays from four-fifths to seven-eighths!

SERVICE INCLUDED

The price of a ticket on a sleeping car is as much as a patron should pay the Pullman Company, and it should carry with it adequate porter service.

A passenger enters a car in spick and span condition as a rule. At the end of the journey, through no fault of his own, he may be dusty, and it becomes the obligation of the Pullman Company to discharge him in as good condition as when he entered the car. The porter is there for this service. Hence, to give him a tip for a "brush," or for any other service he may have rendered to make the use of the company's property comfortable, is a superfluous payment.

The company has a school for training a porter in which he is taught a rigid discipline of attentions to passengers, all of which tend to create in the passenger a sense of obligation toward the porter. Yet not one of these attentions calls for a gratuity if they are examined fairly.

The porter is psychologist enough to know that to create the illusion that he has rendered an extra service is as good for producing a tip as actually to do so. Hence he will come around with a pillow, or shine your shoes during the night unsolicited, or execute some other maneuver that arouses a feeling of obligation. The shining of shoes is outside his ordinary duties, but he has no valid claim for compensation unless specifically requested to perform this service. In his mind is the constant reminder that if the passenger does not make a donation his pay envelope from the company will not meet his bills.

WHAT THE PRESS SAID

Among the many editorial comments that the disclosures of the Walsh Commission evoked is the following from *The St. Louis Republic*:

> The most captious critic of the Pullman Company cannot deny that it merits a unique distinction. Other corporations before now have underpaid their employees . . . but it remained for the Pullman Company to discover how to work on the sympathies of the public in such a manner as to induce that public to make up, by gratuities, for its failure to pay its employees a living wage.
>
> It began this forty years ago, when the "plantation" darky of ante-bellum days was still abroad in the land. It used him, his pathetic history, his peculiar attitude toward the white man, for the accomplishment of its purpose. There at the end of the journey, after the traveler had paid $2, $2.50 or $3 for his berth, stood the porter with his whisk broom and his smile.
>
> And back of him was the pathetic fact, industriously circulated, that "the company" did not pay him enough to live on, so that he was dependent on the gratuities of passengers who

had already paid full price for accommodations and services. We were expected to pay him simply because the Pullman Company didn't. And we paid him. Tens of millions of passengers have paid him millions of dollars.

It wasn't really philanthropy to the porter; it was philanthropy extended to the Pullman Company, which was glad to have the fact of its meanness in its relations to its colored employees—ill-informed of the rights of workingmen and dependent by instinct—published to the world.

It was the Pullman Company which fastened the tipping habit on the American people and they used the negro as the instrument to do it with.

It may be remarked in closing this phase of the discussion that an act of Congress forbidding tips on inter-state carriers would effectually reach the Pullman situation.

XIV
The Government and Tipping

t has been asserted in this discussion that tipping is incompatible with a democratic form of government. Yet we find officials of our Government following the custom and allowing tips as a legitimate item of expense of traveling to be paid out of the public treasury.

FREE AND EQUAL

This state of affairs proves that the work of 1776 and 1787 was limited practically to one phase of democracy, namely, the political. Washington and

101

Jefferson lived in a day when political equality was the passionate ideal. This they and their associates achieved in ample measure. They gave the waiter or the barber or the bootblack an equal voice in government with themselves.

Let those Americans who think that the abolition of tipping would be too radical a step toward social democracy consider how repulsive the attitude of Washington and Jefferson was to the aristocratic thought of their day. No matter what arguments the aristocrats presented against political democracy, their real objection was just this granting of voting equality to persons whom they rated as socially submerged.

But having founded our government upon political democracy, the straight line of development is toward social and industrial democracy, in order to complete the ideal entertained by Washington and Jefferson. That both of these idealists tipped servants and that Washington owned slaves is indisputable, but they left records that prove that they merely "suffered it to be so now." Washington clearly foresaw the trouble in which slavery would involve his country, and would have freed his slaves if he could have done so without precipitating what to him appeared a greater evil in view of all the circumstances of his day.

The Revolutionary period did all that can be asked of one generation when political equality was established. It remains for our generation to finish the work of democracy by establishing social and industrial democracy. The prospect of a street cleaner or your valet being your social and industrial equal may seem either utopian or undesirable, but it must be remembered, as stated, that two centuries ago the thought of granting an equal vote to such persons was precisely as distasteful to the aristocratic mind.

EQUALITY AND UNIFORMITY

Much loose thinking along these lines would be obviated if every one could learn clearly the distinction between "equality" and "uniformity." It is the thought of uniformity that makes most persons belligerent toward democratic impulses in industry or society. They dislike the idea of a dead level of compulsory uniformity. A bootblack and a banker are "equal" in the right to vote, but they are not "uniform" in function or culture. Social democracy will abolish an aristocratic custom like tipping so that every citizen will stand upon an equality of self-respect. It will delete the adjective "menial" from any form of service so that a garbage collector will stand in as honorable a relation to society as a lawyer. But social democracy will not and cannot make naturally uncongenial minds live in a relation of compulsory fellowship.

Thus in the United States we have only one-third of a democracy. The other two-thirds—social and industrial democracy—must be attained before we can consider our government as ideal.

The tipping custom stands squarely in the path of this attainment. The slavery system is not worse in competition with free labor than is the tipping system of compensation. In neither system are values determined by merit or production.

In the list of the 5,000,000 Americans with itching palms were national or city government employees like mail carriers, garbage collectors and policemen. In the larger cities a system of giving gratuities to these and other government employees has grown up that emphasizes the distance we have to travel to attain true democracy.

Any one of these three classes of government employees is paid well for the service he renders. Yet there are mail carriers who will lose a courteous, friendly bearing toward those who fail to "remember" them at Christmas, or at more frequent intervals, or who will actually curtail the service they are paid to render.

MISGUIDED GENEROSITY

There seems to be something about the continual contact of a person serving and a person served that makes the one think the other owes him something on the side. A mail carrier will bring your mail once, twice or several times a day for a period and then enters the feeling that he is entitled to some substantial token of appreciation of his faithful, cheerful service, other than the compensation paid by the government. Often the person being served feels a generous appreciation of good service and bestows a token of it without the person serving having expected or wanted it. The tipping custom is not wholly the outgrowth of greed. It is frequently misguided generosity. Where the error creeps in is in expressing appreciation in terms of money. Self-respect is satisfied with verbal appreciation.

As an employer the government, of all employers, should set an example of true democracy, should practice sound economics and ethics in the relations it permits between its employees and the public. There is no justification from any viewpoint for giving gratuities to public servants. If garbage collectors render slipshod service to citizens who fail to tip them—and they do this regularly—a complaint should bring immediate relief. It does not now because the higher officials are under the same illusion about tipping that envelopes the subordinates.

An inspector of street cleaning in Philadelphia was investigating a complaint against a street sweeper in a residence district. The sweeper told him that he felt the complaint must be ill-founded and that the people in the neighborhood must be satisfied with his sweeping, because he had recently received from residents in one block twenty-one dollars in Christmas tips.

How many public servants in your own neighborhood did you tip last Christmas?

It should not be assumed that the indictment here read is against all mail carriers or garbage collectors, or policemen. With tipping, as with many other abuses "there are more than seven thousand who have not bowed the knee to Baal."

THE GOLDEN RULE

At Christmas the spirit of generosity finds many curious and misdirected expressions. Policemen on certain traffic corners are remembered by many gifts of money and cigars from persons who have no other contact with them than a nod from a limousine as they pass the corner daily. Why should the feeling of appreciation run to thought of money as a token of expression? It is because the persons who give entertain the idea that the policeman is in a stratum of society under them and that, being an underling, his self-respect will not be hurt by offering money. The same persons would not think of offering a friend money and would be insulted if any one offered them money. The golden rule is a dead letter to them.

Some clubs have handled the tipping custom by forbidding gratuities during the year and then allowing the members to contribute to a fund to be divided among the servitors at Christmas. This is a great improvement over the tipping custom but it is still short of the democratic ideal. A servant who is adequately paid for his work throughout the year has no more call upon the generosity of patrons at Christmas than a clerk in a shoe store from whom you purchase shoes four or six times a year.

GOVERNMENT HOTELS

The Government operates hotels in the Canal Zone, and tipping is permitted. Guests who fail to tip are treated by the servitors precisely like they are treated in private hotels, but the writer, who boarded three months in one of the Government hotels in the Canal Zone, during which time he did not tip the waiter, found that a complaint to the manager about poor service would result in the prompt discipline of the offending servitor. This is more than can be said of many privately operated hotels.

In this connection, it is noteworthy that the only whisper of graft in the building of the $400,000,000 canal was the charge made against the purchasing agent of the Commissary that he split commissions with the houses from which he purchased supplies. Splitting commissions is the itching palm in commerce.

It would seem that before passing laws to regulate tipping among citizens, the Government, state and national, should be able to come into court with clean hands. Until the Government rids its service of the spirit of graft the law-makers are beating around the bush.

XV
Laws Against Tipping

Efforts to abolish or regulate the custom of tipping have been made in the Legislatures of practically all of the States. Often after passing legislative barriers the laws have fallen before Executive vetoes, so that scarcely half a dozen States now have statutes on the subject.

The State of Washington adopted a law prohibiting tipping, but it was so generally ignored that the Legislature of 1913 repealed it. This shows that, at first blush, a social custom of long standing has a stronger influence upon the people than a conscientious conviction registered in a new law.

Yet, as abortive as the legal campaign against tipping has been thus far, the constant recurrence of the issue in the Legislatures, and the voluntary attempts at regulation being made by hotels and other public service enterprises, show that the propaganda is making headway and that there are great moral resources in the people ready to be called into action.

CUSTOM ABOVE LAW

The opposition to tipping is unorganized, undisciplined and inarticulate, while the beneficiaries of the custom, with a munificent tribute to nerve activity, are upon a highly efficient basis of operation. Even with a law at his back to stiffen his moral resolution, the average citizen feels more afraid of violating the custom than of violating the law. It is because of the intangible nature of the custom from his viewpoint. A waiter can do so many things to annoy a non-tipping patron that the patron cannot present in the form of a concrete complaint, yet which are quite real and irritating. The upshot is that the patron swallows his conscientious objection to the custom and pays the tribute for fair service.

He knows that a failure to tip means a struggle three times a day in the dining room for his rights and the same struggle at every point of contact with the itching palm. Rather than have his efficiency interfered with by the mental disturbance such rows create, he pays the price. But this type of man will make excellent material in the regular ranks even if he lacks the initiative of a lone hand against big odds. When the movement against tipping reaches the stage where a spokesman and leader is produced, all the latent opposition will spring into effective coöperation.

THE IOWA LAW

Some of the laws are aimed exclusively at the takers of tips and others at the givers as well. The Iowa law is in the first class, as follows:

> Sec. 5028-u. Accepting or Soliciting Gratuity or Tip. Every employee of any hotel, restaurant, barber shop, or other public place, and every employee of any person, firm partnership, or corporation, or of any public service corporation engaged in the transportation of passengers in this state, who shall accept or solicit any gratuity, tip or other thing of value or of valuable consideration, from any guest or patron, shall be guilty of a misdemeanor, and upon conviction thereof shall be fined not less than five dollars, or more than twenty-five dollars, or be imprisoned in the county jail for a period not exceeding thirty days.

This law makes the mere acceptance of a tip illegal and it also heads off any attempt to circumvent the law on a technicality by prohibiting the acceptance of "other thing of value or of valuable consideration."

THE WISCONSIN BILL

The Wisconsin bill, which the Governor vetoed on the ground that it curtailed "personal liberty" was intended to penalize the giving of the tip, and was worded as follows:

> Sec. 45751. Every employee of any hotel, restaurant or public place and every employee of any person, firm or of any public service corporation engaged in the transportation of passengers or the furnishing of food, lodging and other accommodations to the public in this state who shall receive or solicit any gratuity or tip from any guest or patron shall be guilty of a misdemeanor. Every person who shall give or offer any gratuity or tip to any person or employee prohibited from receiving or soliciting the same by the provisions of this section shall also be guilty of a misdemeanor.
>
> Every hotel, restaurant, firm and public service corporation engaged in the transportation of passengers or in furnishing food or lodging or other accommodations to the public shall keep a copy of this law posted in a conspicuous place in such hotel and restaurant and in the dining or sleeping cars of any firm or public service corporation mentioned in this section. Any persons violating any of the provisions of this section shall be guilty of a misdemeanor and upon conviction shall be fined not less than five dollars, nor more than twenty-five dollars, or by imprisonment in the county jail not to exceed thirty days.

The demand for this bill was so strong among the members of the Legislature that it almost was passed over the Governor's veto. The provision that a copy of the law must be posted in the places where the public comes into contact with the itching palm is a most essential one. It reassures patrons to see it and gives them a present stimulus for standing upon their right to good service for one payment.

THE COURTS AND TIPPING

The courts, in declaring such laws unconstitutional have proceeded upon the common law right of one citizen to give away his goods or property in the form of money to any other citizen. A tip, the judges say, represents a gift within the meaning of this common law right. But the instances of such altruism are exceedingly rare.

Even the judges who so decide know that the tips they give are not bona fide gifts out of the goodness of a generous heart. Tips are given, by the devotees of the custom, from a sense of obligation. They pretend to feel that the servitor actually has rendered a service for which the tip is payment. The proof of this is found in the fact that such persons never go about giving money gifts indiscriminately. Their gifts are exclusively to the employees of public service enterprises, showing that no thought of charity or generosity enters their minds.

The courts some day will come to the conclusion that a gift of money to any serving person is a special relation that is subject to the police power of the State. The special circumstances surrounding the gift will be taken into consideration. Then it will be seen that the gift was made for something the patron did not receive; for something for which he is required to pay twice and that the motives of the gift were pride, or fear or a sense of obligation falsely aroused.

While the courts are so scrupulous in preserving the common law right to make gifts, they might give consideration to the equally indubitable right of a patron to receive full value for his money, and to receive such value for one payment.

It may be, that to write an anti-tipping law that will stand the test of judges educated in the old school of thought about gratuities, legislators will have to approach the subject from this viewpoint of preserving a patron's common law right to satisfactory service for one payment. For instance, a law specifically defining the right of a patron to have food served, or to use a hotel room or sleeping car facilities, in short to patronize any public service place, with only one charge, and that to be paid exclusively to the proprietor, might strike an effective blow at "the universal heart of Flunkyism."

The courts will assert that the foregoing right exists without a special statute, and it does. Still the average citizen does not think of instituting a suit against a hotel, or swearing out a warrant against the manager or an employee to enforce his common law right to service at one price. If there is a specific statute against tipping there is a more tangible inducement to stand up for one's rights and there is more likelihood that redress will be granted. The defense of tipping on the "personal liberty" plea, like the defense of the liquor business on the same plea, will grow feebler and feebler until judges cease to take the aristocratic viewpoint.

THE SOUTH CAROLINA LAW

The South Carolina law goes a step ahead of either the Iowa law or the Wisconsin bill in the provision that the employer shall not permit the custom of tipping, in addition to provisions prohibiting the giving or receiving of tips by patrons or employees. The law follows:

> It shall be unlawful in this State for any hotel, restaurant, café, dining car company, railroad companies, sleeping car company or barber shop to knowingly allow any person in its employ to receive any gratuity commonly known as a tip, from any patron or passenger, and it shall be unlawful for any patron of any hotel, restaurant, café, dining car or for any passenger on any railroad train or sleeping car to give any employee any such gratuity and it shall be unlawful for any employee of any hotel, restaurant, café, dining car, railroad company, sleeping car company or barber shop to receive any such gratuity.
>
> By 'gratuity' or 'tip' as used in this Act, is to mean any extra compensation of any kind,

which any hotel, restaurant, café, dining car, railroad company, sleeping car company or barber shop manager, officer or any agent thereof in charge of the same, allows to be given to any employee and is not a part of the regular charge of the hotel, restaurant, café, dining car, railroad company, sleeping car company or barber shop, for any part of service rendered, or a part of the service which by contract it is under duty to render. No company or incorporation shall evade this Act by adding to the regular charge, directly or indirectly, anything intended for or to be used or to be given away as a gratuity or tip to the employee. All charges must be made by the company or proprietor in good faith as a charge for the service it renders, inclusive of the service which it furnishes through employees.

Each hotel shall post a copy of this Act in each room and each restaurant, café and barber shop shall post at least two copies of this Act in two conspicuous places in their places of business, and each railroad company shall post two copies of this Act in their waiting rooms and passenger rooms at passenger stations in cities of three thousand inhabitants or more, and each sleeping car and dining car shall have posted therein at least one copy of this Act.

Any person or corporation failing to post as required shall be fined not less than ten dollars for such failure and each day of failure shall constitute a separate and distinct offense and any person violating any of the other provisions of this Act shall be subject to a fine of not less than ten dollars or more than one hundred dollars, or be imprisoned for not exceeding thirty days.

This South Carolina law was an evident effort to cover the custom of tipping in a manner that would permit of no evasions. It defines a "tip" and prohibits surreptitious gratuities and makes employer, employee and patron equally liable to prosecution. Yet, it falls short of an ideal law because its operations are limited to seven places frequented by the public and does not cover private places where the itching palm flourishes, such as apartment houses and boarding houses.

To stop tipping in hotels, restaurants, cafés, dining cars, railroad stations and cars, sleeping cars or barber shops will be a long stride in the right direction, but the need of stopping tipping to messenger boys, janitors and other employees of apartment houses, maids and waitresses in boarding houses, garbage collectors, mail carriers and policemen among government employees, trunk transfermen, guides, steamship employees and others too numerous to cite, is fully as urgent.

The Ideal Law

The ideal act will be evolved through these repeated approximations and through experience. In a broad outline it must include (1) a clear definition of a tip, (2) a statement of a patron's right to service for one payment exclusively to the proprietor, (3) a prohibition against subterfuges in the charges whereby patrons may give tips, (4) the wages paid by an employer to be considered as presumptive evidence of his attitude toward tipping, (5) a requirement that employers shall give patrons a definite understanding of the service to which they are entitled, (6) any actual extra service to be compensated for direct to employer after being appraised and charged for by the employer, (7) the giving of money or gifts to employees to be taken out of the class of "charity" and "personal liberty," (8) the employer, the employee and the patron to be subject to the same penalty for violating the law and the conviction of any one of the three to be followed automatically by the conviction of the other two for the same offense, (9) the law to be applicable to any employer and any employee in any relation with the public or with individuals, in private home or public place, (10) a prohibition against operating any convenience for the public in which the rate of payment shall be left to the whim of the patron, such as cloak rooms, the tariffs to be displayed and exacted impartially of every patron if the employer assumes that patrons must pay extra for the service, (11) an adequate provision for acquainting patrons with the law through posting it or otherwise directing their attention to it, (12) the granting of licenses to operate public service places only upon condition that gratuities are not to be permitted, directly or indirectly, (13) the granting to a patron who has been denied fair service of redress in addition to the punishment of the guilty employee and employer, (14) an adequate scale of penalties, fine or imprisonment for any violation of any part of the law.

It is not presumed that if a law were drawn to embody the foregoing provisions that the tipping custom would be strangled. Only actual tests in the courts will produce the ultimate intent. Of course, if employers and employees and patrons were actuated by a desire to maintain their relations upon a basis of self-respect so circumstantial a law would be unnecessary, but many of them are not thus actuated and a minute restraint will be imperative at the outset and until a normal ideal of democracy is cultivated.

The Nebraska Act

The bill introduced in the 1915 session of the Nebraska Legislature does not penalize the patron for giving gratuities and seems to be aimed at the practice of "split commissions" as well as at tipping. It has a maximum fine of one hundred dollars, or imprisonment of sixty days and the employers only are specified for conviction. The act follows:

> No employee or servant shall accept, obtain or agree to accept, or attempt to obtain, from any person, for himself or for any other person, any gift, gratuity or consideration as an inducement to perform or as a reward for having performed any duty or service for which such employee or servant has been employed or is to be paid by the employer or master, firm or corporation of such employee or servant.

No employer or master, firm or corporation shall permit or allow any of his or their employees or servants to solicit or to accept any gift, gratuity or consideration as an inducement to perform or as a reward for having performed any duty or service for which such employee or servant has been or is to be paid by such employer or master, firm or corporation.

Each and every employer or master, firm or corporation who carries on business as the keeper of a hotel, inn, restaurant, café, place for the sale of alcoholic beverages, barber shop or place for polishing boots and shoes, or who operates a railroad dining, buffet, sleeping or parlor car, shall post up or cause to be posted up in at least two conspicuous places in the premises in which such business is carried on, or in such car, a notice that tipping, or the giving of any gift or gratuity to any servant or employee, is forbidden under penalty of fine or imprisonment.

No employer or master, firm or corporation shall give or agree to give or offer to any employee or servant any gift, gratuity or consideration as an inducement to perform or as a reward for having performed any duty or service for which such employer or servant has been or is to be paid by the employer, master, firm or corporation employing such servants.

Each and every employer, master, firm or corporation who shall violate any of the provisions herein made shall be deemed guilty of a misdemeanor and upon conviction shall be liable in each and every case to a fine of not less than ten dollars nor more than one hundred dollars, or to imprisonment in the county jail of the proper county not less than ten nor more than sixty

days, or to both such fine and imprisonment, at
the discretion of the court.

THE TENNESSEE LAW

The Tennessee law was adopted upon the especial
solicitation of the traveling salesmen of the State.
These men live constantly in touch with the itching
palm and find the tribute not only burdensome to
themselves but to their employers. The act is much
like the South Carolina law, and a notable feature
is Section 6:

> That it shall be the duty of the circuit judges and
> the courts of like jurisdiction to especially call
> the attention of the grand jury to the provisions
> of this act at each term of the court.

The foregoing provision makes it certain that,
even if patrons are timid about obeying the law and
if employers and employees disregard it, the fight
against the custom will go right on, just as does the
fight against bootlegging after saloons have been
banished from a city. The Tennessee law also has a
more elaborate scale of fines, as the following section shows:

> Be it further enacted that any hotel, restaurant,
> café, barber shop, dining car, railroad or sleep-
> ing car company, and the manager, officer or
> agent of the same in charge, violating this act
> or wilfully allowing the same to be violated in
> any way, shall each be subject to a penalty of

not less than $10 nor more than $50 for each tip allowed to be given. If any person shall give an employee any gratuity or tip each person shall be subject to a fine of not more than $25 and not less than $5 for each offense. If any of the above employees shall receive a gratuity or tip he or she shall be subject to a fine of not more than $25 nor less than $5 for each offense. Should any hotel, restaurant, café, barber shop, dining car, railroad company or sleeping car company fail, neglect or refuse to post notice of this act as required herein, such hotel, restaurant, café, barber shop, dining car, railroad or sleeping car company shall be subject to a fine not to exceed $100 for each day it shall fail.

Naturally if this law is enforced with any fidelity by the grand juries, not to mention such actions as may be instituted by the public, tipping in Tennessee in the specified public service place will become extinct, or assume a guise not covered by the law. But if tipping is restrained only in the seven places enumerated and allowed to be practiced unrestrained everywhere else, only a limited industrial democracy will be attained, and the part of the custom left alive will spread by its own insidious processes to the places preëmpted.

The Illinois Compromise

When the public conscience is fully aroused to the need of stifling this custom, the legal mind will be able to draw up a law that will prevent tipping anywhere and under any circumstances. The Illinois law is a particular example of a half-way measure in that it seeks only to prohibit the practice of leasing tipping concessions to employees.

> That it shall be unlawful for the owner, proprietor, lessee, superintendent, manager or agent in any hotel, restaurant, eating house, barber shop, theatre, store building, office building, factory, railroad, street railroad, fair ground, baseball or football ground, hall used for public meetings or entertainments, or any other building, office, or space which is a place of public accommodation or public resort, to rent, lease or permit to be used any part, space or portion thereof, for any trade, calling or occupation, or for the exercise of any privilege by any person, company, partnership or corporation for the purpose of accepting, demanding or receiving, directly or indirectly, from the customers, patrons or people who frequent such places of public accommodation or public resort, gratuities or donations, commonly called tips, in addition to the regular, ordinary and published rate of charge for work performed, materials furnished or services rendered, provided, that nothing in this section contained shall be construed to prohibit any employee or servant from accepting or receiving gratuities or donations commonly called tips, if such gratuities or donations are not accounted for, paid over, or delivered, directly, or indirectly, in whole or in part, to any person, company, partnership or corporation, but are retained by such employee

or servant, as and for his absolute and individual property.

Any lease, contract, agreement or understanding entered into in violation of the provisions of section 1 of this act shall be absolutely void.

Any person, company, partnership or corporation or any officer or agent thereof, violating
the provisions of this act shall be deemed guilty
of a misdemeanor and upon conviction shall be
fined in any sum not exceeding ten thousand
dollars for each and every offense, and, in addition thereto such person, officer or agent, in
the discretion of the court, be sentenced to the
county jail not less than three months and not
more than one year.

Legalized Robbery

This Illinois law is an instance of an American
Commonwealth specifically and deliberately rec-
ognizing tipping as legal and right. It turns loose
the tip-pirates upon the public with full govern-
mental sanction, but stipulates that in their pira-
cy they shall not organize into a trust, as they had
done in Chicago and in all large cities.

The Illinois law can be commended to the extent
that it seeks to break up the organized traffic in
tips, but its recognition of tipping on an unorganized basis is equivalent to the action of some European governments in paying out of their treasuries
tribute to the Barbary pirates for the privilege of
sailing the high seas. Thomas Jefferson's democ-

racy rebelled at this and he freed the whole world from the outrageous custom.

IN MASSACHUSETTS

Massachusetts has a law to prohibit the corrupt influencing of agents, employees or servants, but it is aimed specially at the practice of "splitting commissions" and does not operate to restrain tipping in the State. A salesman sometimes will offer to give a buyer a bonus or part of his commission if an order is placed, and this practice is causing the business world considerable thought, as employers realize that a buyer who will accept favors from salesmen will not exercise unbiased judgment. It is the itching palm a plane above tipping owing to the larger amount involved, and is akin to the graft of public officials. The law follows:

> Whoever corruptly gives, offers or promises to an agent, employee or servant any gift or gratuity whatever, with intent to influence his action in relation to his principal's, employer's or master's business; or an agent, employee or servant who corruptly requests or accepts a gift or gratuity or a promise to make a gift or to do an act beneficial to himself under an agreement or with an understanding that he shall act in any particular manner in relation to his principal's, employer's or master's business; or an agent, employee or servant, who, being authorized to procure materials, supplies or other articles either by purchase or contract for his principal,

employer or master, or to employ service or labor for his principal, employer or master receives, directly or indirectly, for himself or for another, a commission, discount or bonus from the person who makes such sale or contract, or furnishes such materials, supplies or other articles, or from a person who renders such service or labor; and any person who gives or offers such an agent, employee or servant such commission, discount or bonus, shall be punished by a fine of not less than ten dollars nor more than five hundred dollars, or by such fine and by imprisonment for not more than one year.

Although the Arkansas and Mississippi laws against tipping are not mentioned, a comprehensive idea of the extent and nature of the opposition to the custom in the United States is presented in the review of the bills introduced in or enacted by the Legislatures of Iowa, Wisconsin, South Carolina, Nebraska, Tennessee, Illinois, and Massachusetts. All the other States have no laws against tipping. Considering the fact that no organization has been formed to agitate for this reform, these spontaneous State efforts are significant.

XVI

Samuel Gompers on Tipping

abor has the strongest interest of any element of citizens for seeing the 5,000,000 men, women and children with itching palms elevated to a normal plane of self-respect. For nothing in America more certainly promotes class distinctions than tipping. It is essentially aristocratic, and labor has attained its widest development in democracy.

WAITERS AGAINST THE TIP CUSTOM

Occasionally waiters and some other workers in a serving capacity have attempted to organize and

127

place their work upon the wage-system, rather than the combination wage-and-tip system, or the strictly tip system, now existing. In New York in 1913 the waiters struck for higher wages and serious riots occurred before they capitulated to the old system. The hotels preferred the tipping system because it throws the cost of waiter hire upon the public, whereas, an adequate wage system would necessitate a readjustment of their business.

Even where the waiters and barbers have organized they have not always shown aggressive efforts to abolish or regulate the tipping custom. The barbers, for instance, are highly organized, and any real desire upon their part to abolish the custom would be followed by immediate reform. But it is evident that the tipping system of compensation is attractive to many persons who serve the public because it yields more pay than a wage system. In the higher strata of workers particularly the tips are so large as to stupefy moral sense, and this minority dominates the majority by setting a standard of "proper" social usage.

A Labor Leader on Tips

Mr. Samuel Gompers, president of the American Federation of Labor, has opposed tipping as an irregular form of compensation, and in response to an inquiry for his opinion he inclosed a letter he had written to the manager of the Hotel Stowell, in Los Angeles, where a non-tipping rule is enforced.

Hotel Stowell, Los Angeles, Calif.

Replying to your letter of November 28th I beg to say that I found your hotel and service eminently satisfactory and was particularly pleased with the rule you have enforced as to no tipping.

While, of course, I have followed the usual custom of giving tips, yet I have maintained the principle of tipping to be unwise and that it tends to lessen the self-respect of a man who accepts a tip.

Very truly yours,
(Signed) SAMUEL GOMPERS,
American Federation of Labor.

This letter is interesting as revealing the attitude of many prominent Americans, namely, that while they conform to the custom rather than be subjected to insults, annoyance and poor service, they really consider it inimical to self-respect.

EUROPEAN TIPS

Mr. Gompers in his letter said: "You have my permission to quote my opinion upon this subject in any way that you may desire," and gave permission to have reproduced here the chapter in his book, *Labor in Europe and America*, which deals with tipping in Europe, as he encountered it in his investigations of labor conditions. The chapter is entitled "Nuisances of European Travel" and is as follows:

Having in previous letters given my impressions with regard to matters of more serious import, I wish to say something about the almost hourly sufferings of American travelers in Europe from mosquito bites. To the sharp probes from these insects, with the resultant pain, fever and disgust, the traveler is obliged to submit continually—at hotels and restaurants, on the railroad and often elsewhere—as he goes seeing the sights. To illustrate: our party on arriving at The Hague engaged two mosquitoes in the form of station porters to carry our hand-baggage to the bus of the Hotel Blank, waiting at the curb of the station exit. The station porters passed the valises over to the hotel bus porter at a point just within the station door. Nip! nip! by the two station porters.

NIP! NIP!

When we arrived at the hotel door both the bus porter and the bus driver asked me for what they regarded as their due drop of blood. Nip! nip! Within the door of the hotel the manager informed us that all his rooms had been engaged by telegraph, but that he could give us good rooms at a clean hotel near by, and we took them. Two hotel porters who had carried our bits of hand-baggage into the hotel lobby asked me, as soon as the hotel manager had turned his back, for their tribute. Nip! nip! Yet another porter, after taking the things a few steps down the street to the other hotel stood by in the hallway and waited to give us his nip. Seven gouges of silver change out of my pocket before we reached our rooms! But the probes of the mosquito swarms of this hotel reached even further. The little hotel charged us Hotel Blank rates for our rooms, about double what would have been asked had we gone there direct and bargained for accommodations. And the dinner at the Hotel Blank cost us half a florin apiece more than the price set down in the guide-book. In this incident the reader sees some, but not all, of the methods of stinging which the hotel mosquitoes practice.

In Berlin, just at the moment of our departure, the porter, the gold-laced and brass-buttoned dignitary who browbeats lamblike guests at European hotel entrances, handed us our laundry bill, every article of which was charged double to treble New York prices. In Vienna, tired of blood-letting to each mosquito separately in the group of servants always assembled about the door upon our departure—'the review' they themselves call this evolution—I drew the manager aside and said: 'I understand that there is a way of giving tips to all hands through the management.' (One bleeding as it were.) 'How much extra shall I give you?' He replied: 'Twenty per cent. of your bill.'

"Bribe and Be Happy"

I was rather tickled than bitten the first time I got a nip in a European railway train. One of our party suggested that as the second-class places were crowded we should go into a first-class compartment and await results. When the conductor, in his jim-dandy uniform, came along, he was handed our second-class tickets and a mark—a silver coin worth a paltry twenty-five cents. And he took our tickets and passed on without seeing for what class they called. The vast possibilities of cheaply purchased privileges on future trips acted as a palliative to this little sting. And the thought of what might happen if the traveler in America should try to overcome the virtue of one of our express-train conductors with a 'quarter' brought all our party to see the circumstance from a humorous point of view. Truth to relate, it marked the beginning of a custom we followed—since we learned that it was general—of buying our way past any obstacle that appeared to interrupt the smoothness or comfort of our daily progress. With a little silver we henceforth obtained concessions from grand-looking policemen, soldiers on guard, vergers in churches, museum custodians. It is a common custom for conductors on street cars in Continental Europe to hold out their hands to receive as a tip any small change due, but first handed over to the passenger. You may have your choice in European travel: Bribe and be otherwise happy and free, or virtuously decline to bribe and be snubbed, ordered about and forbidden to see things.

BORDERS ON BLACKMAIL

The tipping system, bad as it is becoming in America, is in Europe universal and accepted by all classes of travelers as an inevitable nuisance. It often borders on blackmail. Tippers go raving mad in recounting their wrongs under the tyrannies of the system, the newspapers by turn rail or make merry over it, the hotel keepers and other employers of the class have their excuse that they pay wages to their servants—but the tipping goes on forever. Why is it? Who is to blame?

These questions I have asked representative waiters—for representatives these men have, many of them being organized into benefit societies and a small proportion in a sort of trade union. But one answer was given. The system is detestable to every man and woman of the serving class possessing the least degree of self-respect. It is demoralizing to all who either give or receive tips. The real beneficiaries of the system are the employers. An end to it, with a fair standard of wages, would be a boon of the first order to employees, a means of compelling hotel proprietors to put their business on a basis of fair dealing, and an incalculable aid to the tranquillity and pleasure of the general public.

Moral Pirates

"I have often talked over the system of tipping with my fellow waiters," said an educated man of the calling, when I brought up the subject to him. (Parenthetically, perhaps, I should say here that since this man speaks fluently and writes correctly four languages, has traveled much and observed well on the great tourist routes of the world, has studied some of the serious works of writers on sociology, and has, withal, acquired agreeable manners, he may be called educated. Without doubt, had he a few thousands of vulgar dollars he might buy himself a title as Baron and marry in our best society; but he is above that; he has a craving for walking in the light of truth.) "All of us would like to see the system abolished," he assured me, "except a small minority who in their moral make-up resemble pirates, and who cruise in places where riches abound. But the whole situation is one in which reform is most difficult.

Among the people who patronize hotels and restaurants there is a considerable element that, either for a week of frolic or during their lifelong holiday, are regardless of the value of their tips, and through their vanity enjoy throwing away a percentage of their ready money. Then, also, are those grateful for the little kindly attentions which a good waiter or porter knows how to bestow. As for the proprietors and managers, their business is based on tips as one of the considerable forms of revenue. For instance, in many German hotels the waiters are obliged to give the cashier five or more marks additional on every hundred marks of checks. In Austria, at the larger restaurants the customers tip three persons after a meal—the head-waiter who collects the payments, the waiter who serves and the piccolo or beer-boy. The hotel management sells to the head-waiter the monopoly privilege of the tips. The head-waiter then provides the newspapers and magazines on file, the city directories, time-tables and other books of reference called for by patrons, and a part of the outfit of the waiters. Of course, it is an old and true story, that in the big restaurants of Paris, and to-day of other cities and fashionable watering-places, the waiters pay so much cash a day for their jobs. The pestering of guests to buy drinks comes, not so much from commissions, as from orders of the management that the custom of drinking at meals must be encouraged.

In Germany it is usual at the larger restaurants to add half a mark to the cost of a meal if the guest drinks plain water only.

Too Many Servants

European hotels generally take on more servants than are necessary. It makes a showing of being prepared for big business. Then the servants must redouble their artful moves to extort tips. Porters not infrequently work without salary at all. Chambermaids, who are paid by the month, receive absurdly low pay. Financing a hotel or restaurant is based on the tips as a margin yielding on the average a fixed amount. To make them reach the required sum all the employees are obliged to maneuver so as to put up a showing of earning the traveler's extra silver pieces. Coppers rarely are expected as tips now. It has become common for railway station porters to demand half a franc for what once brought them a few sous or pfennigs.

One outcome of running a hotel on the tipping system developed to the point of bamboozling or worrying the guests out of petty extras at every turn is that each year there is an emigration of European waiters to America to get places in hotels taken by European managers, who, depending upon their servants to work the system at its worst for the guests, can make a business pay both manager and landlord, where an American manager, paying wages, would fail. While shop-keepers have in the course of time been forced to adopt the one-price system, the drift in the hotel business has been continuously away from the *per diem* rate. Another point—the big tourist agencies for European travel are certainly in some sort of partnership with the hotels for which they sell coupon tickets. Those on the inside of the hotel business in Europe know that these hotels are patronized largely by Americans, spendthrifts on their trip staying a few days at a time and usually speaking English only, and therefore disinclined to hunt up stopping-places for themselves. Hence at such hotels there is a harvest for everybody—a situation which eventually leads to bad food, bad cooking, bad service, and a hold-up at every turn of the guest."

A Sorry Business

In going over the possible method of a change for the better in this sorry business, my waiter friend said that first of all he believed that a big trade union must be formed of hotel help. Tipping must give way to fair wages. The public could give its share of assistance. He recommended that the guests at either hotels or restaurants should follow these rules, notes of which were taken on the spot. "Patronize, whenever possible, the hotels and eating houses where tips are forbidden; there are such places in England and on the continent. Refuse importunities for tips, either through words or 'hanging around,' where there has been no service. Where, for your own comfort you feel constrained to tip give the bare minimum. Whenever possible do not tip at all."

He added, and I felt that he had me also in mind, "Some easy-going natured people believe that they tip the nearest itching palm to them because of their sympathy with the poor. Reflection should teach them that there can sometimes be real charity without public demonstration."

True, church people might, with this purpose, give through their own congregational agencies. In London, the American traveler wishing to do the best with his withheld tip-appropriation, might send it to the Westminster Children's Aid Society; In Rome, to the Society for the Prevention of Cruelty to Animals; In Berlin, to the semi-public lodging houses. Everywhere, trade-unionists can always give first to the genuine and pressing claims of their own organizations. But, of course, if the tipper, gives, not from motives of good-heartedness, but mere vanity, all advice is thrown away on him. The hotel keeper will continue growing rich on him and despising him. Other folks in Europe may have good reason to tell him, what a plain spoken Swiss citizen told a friend of mine: "You Americans with your dirty dollars are ruining my country."

Vanity, All Is Vanity!

Mr. Gompers in this chapter from his book has shed much light on the ethics, economics and psychology of tipping. The deliberate, shameless exploitation of the public by employers and employees is revealed. No ground to stand upon is left to the tip givers except vanity, and the pernicious influence of the custom, to patron, employee and employer, is so unmistakable that the doom of the custom is as certain as was slavery, when the American conscience once squarely faces the issue.

Hotel and restaurant managers in our cities have employed European waiters upon the theory that the native American has too much independence and self-respect. The European waiters have multiplied the tip-giving propensity in America and have established their undemocratic sovereignty over our public hospitality. Inasmuch as a certain element of Americans think that the last word in social propriety originates in Europe, when these European servitors are transplanted, gold lace and all, to America, they hasten to enlarge their tips to the point which they assume these servitors consider "proper."

The astonishing feature of the European situation is that the European patrons of hotels do not themselves tip within a tenth of the largess bestowed by American tourists. The American tourist is fair game to the European hotel, which trebles its regular rates the moment he appears. A native of the country, however, can have identically the same accommodations for one-third of the American's bill, and his tips are a bagatelle in comparison.

The situation may be changed by an organization of employees, but reform will come most speedily whenever the public, which pays the bill, decides to withhold the tribute.

XVII
The Way Out

Summarizing the case against tipping, the following facts stand out prominently:

1. Flunkyism is rampant in the American democracy and this aristocratic influence is undermining republican ideals and institutions.

2. Flunkyism, in the form of tipping, is kept alive by the courts on the plea of "personal liberty."

3. Tipping nowadays is of precisely the same morality as paying tribute to the Barbary Pirates was in Jefferson's day, which the American conscience finally abolished.

139

4. On the economic side, tipping is wrong because it is payment for no service, or double payment for one service; thereby causing the exchange of wealth without a mutual gain.

5. Tipping is ethically wrong because one person accepts payment for a service not rendered, or for a service which the employer already has paid to have performed. And because gratuities destroy self-respect.

6. The hold which tipping has upon the public is due to unscrupulous appeals to generosity, pride and fear of violating conventional social usage.

7. The public is exploited deliberately through books on social propriety which emphasize the custom, or which advise conformity thereto for the sake of peace and comfort.

8. The exploitation of the public is aided by the visualization of the custom in moving pictures and on the stage where it is treated humorously.

9. Employees defend tipping upon the ground that it compensates them for extra services not covered in their wages. An examination of individual instances shows this contention to be false in a vast majority of the number examined.

10. Employers defend the custom on the ground that the public insists upon giving gratuities and they must face competition based upon that condition. But it is shown that employers openly profit by the custom and secretly encourage it.

11. One metropolitan hotel has blazed the way to reform by guaranteeing that its guests will not

be annoyed or neglected if tips are not given. This partial step toward the abolition of the custom is possible everywhere if employers are sincere in their profession of antipathy for the custom.

12. Our democratic government permits its officers and employees to accept gratuities, thereby stultifying the spirit of the Declaration of Independence and the Constitution.

13. The conscience of the people as reflected in the laws adopted or offered against tipping is sound and needs only to be led to an adequate expression. There are abundant indications of a widespread distaste for the custom but the sentiment is unorganized and inarticulate.

14. The head of the labor movement in America declares that tipping is undesirable as a system of compensation for employees and destroys the self-respect of those who give or receive the gratuities.

15. A national organization of those interested in this reform should be brought into being with effective state auxiliaries.

BETTER ORGANIZATION NEEDED

The last proposition constitutes "the way out" of the present undesirable situation. When it is remembered that the anti-tipping propaganda heretofore has lacked organization and direction it is not surprising that the laws adopted against the custom and the spasmodic public irritation over it have fizzled out. With the same organization behind this movement that has been given to the anti-saloon movement, or the suffrage movement, tipping would be vanquished in an astonishingly short time.

There is no doubt there is sufficient latent opposition to tipping to form the basis of an anti-tipping organization. It may be called "The American Anti-Tipping Association," or by any other name, and it should embrace in its membership not only those who are opposed to giving tips, but those servants and workers who are opposed to receiving tips, and also all other persons of any race or creed whose conception of true Americanism does not include approval of this custom.

Not a War Against Persons

The object of such an organization should not be to wage war on persons, but on a custom. There is no need for hostility against waiters, barbers, porters and the like as a class. Many of these heartily oppose the custom and will join in a movement to eradicate it. Hence, the campaign should be to readjust the basis of compensation of those who serve the public so that self-respect may be preserved all around. Nothing less than a fair wage as a substitute for the present tipping system of compensation would be considered.

Having made the foregoing point clear at the outset, much resentment among servitors would be eliminated. No one has a desire to deprive a waiter of an adequate compensation, but no one has a desire to give him an excessive compensation through gratuities, or a compensation which depresses his self-respect in the manner of receiving and humiliates the patron in the manner of giving.

Employers would need to be informed, too, that the campaign against tipping is not to throw an unjust burden of operating expense upon them. It will indeed deprive them of any revenues which they should not, economically or ethically, receive from the public through gratuities to employees. The substitution of a wage scale will be attended by economic changes which at first may cause some unsettled conditions, but this is inevitable when an unsound practice has been allowed to grow unrestrained in the business world.

PUBLIC OPINION

One of the first aims of such an organization would be to bring public opinion to bear upon city, state and national governments to inspire them to clean house in regard to tipping. No government employee should be permitted to accept any compensation other than his salary or wages from the government. Mail carriers, policemen, garbage collectors, guides and other government employees are paid adequately and gratuities to them from the public are indefensible, in any country, and supremely so in the American democracy.

The public, of course, will need to revise its attitude toward these and all persons who serve them. The feeling that a traffic policeman whom you pass in your automobile every day should be remembered with a gift of money or anything else substantial at Christmas, or upon any other occasion is false sentiment. He is due nothing except courtesy all the time from the public, which, through taxes, already has provided his compensation. The feeling that a mail carrier whom you see daily, or a garbage collector, must be similarly remembered is equally false sentiment. The ideal is a relation in which patron and employee, public and government employee, entertain mutual opinions of self-respect, and regardless of how distasteful this may be to class sense, or aristocratic impulses, it is the American standard and the right standard.

PROMOTING LEGISLATION

An organization opposed to tipping would have as its further objects the promotion of legislation against the custom and the protection of the public in the enjoyment of its rights at law. If so many States have adopted laws as a spontaneous expression of Americanism, it may be assumed that with organized public sentiment, and educated public sentiment all the States will get in line. There will be abundant financial resources behind such an organization. Those who oppose tipping have been silent but they have felt keenly and will contribute liberally toward the advancement of the cause. And when such an organization actually proves its efficacy in protecting the public, its ranks will be augmented overwhelmingly.

The protection hinted at is the kind that would take up specific instances of neglect of patrons who do not give tips. Thus, if a member should be neglected or insulted in a hotel after he had failed to bestow a gratuity, the organization, upon investigation, would assume the task of correcting the situation at law. Even where there is no statute against tipping, the common law guarantees the right of a patron to fair and equal service, and the organization could enforce this right in the courts.

Naturally, great care and good judgment would be needed to prevent an injustice to proprietors and employees. Often patrons exact more service than they are entitled to, and in such a situation the organization would be ranged on the side of the employee. Those who desire a condition where they may run rough-shod over servitors have a mistaken idea of the anti-tipping ideal. The employer is required to have employees who will give cheerful, adequate service, but within the limits of reason, and the selfish, domineering, patron is an evil which must be restrained as effectually as the waiter who surreptitiously insults patrons who do not tip.

To Prevent Complaint

Surveying the vast field of tipping one may wonder how any organization could offer protection to the numberless patrons who might complain. The answer is that the organization would be as widespread as the custom. Every town and city would have its local organization with an attorney to prosecute violations. But it is reasonable to presume that when public opinion is once thoroughly aroused and organized, and a few prosecutions have been successful, that employers and employees, who do not voluntarily reform their practices, will see the light.

As deep-rooted as the custom seems, it really rests on insecure foundations and will crumble before any real attack. The average American, be he barber, waiter or porter, has enough inherent understanding of democracy to know that the custom is wrong. He "will get his" as long as an easy-going public will stand for the exaction, but will not be a formidable opponent. The imported European waiter will present more obstinate fondness for the custom, having been nurtured in the aristocratic school, but his opposition can be handled.

The most difficult type will be the class of patrons who delight in playing the rôle of Lady Bountiful or Gentleman Generous. Their pride will be restrained from buying servility from other Americans. And wealthy proprietors, who cater to this class and the intermediate class which ape the "smart set," will cling to the custom because of their pecuniary interest therein. But the average American and his vigorous sense of democracy will be adequate to the task of controlling all elements adverse to the republic.

The campaign against tipping is much more than a purpose to save the money given in gratuities. Its idealism aims to reach the very pinnacle of republican society—the destiny toward which 1776 started us. The mountain peaks of pride will have to be pulled down and the valleys of false humility will have to be lifted up, while the impulses to greed and avarice will have to be rebuked until every American can say:

> If I must build my pride upon another man's
>   humility,
> I will not be proud;
> If I must build my strength upon another man's
>   weakness,
> I will not be strong;
> If I must build my success upon another man's
>   failure,
> I will not succeed!

Index